Just Peace

Remember to play after every storm.

Love,
Mattie

2004 MDA National Goodwill Ambassador

Other Books by Mattie J.T. Stepanek

Heartsongs

Journey Through Heartsongs

Hope Through Heartsongs

Celebrate Through Heartsongs

Loving Through Heartsongs

Reflections of a Peacemaker:
A Portrait Through Heartsongs

Just
Peace:
A Message of Hope

Mattie J.T. Stepanek
with Jimmy Carter

Edited by Jennifer Smith Stepanek

Andrews McMeel
Publishing
Kansas City

06 07 08 09 10 RR2 10 9 8 7 6 5 4 3 2 1

ISBN-13: 978-0-7407-5712-9
ISBN-10: 0-7407-5712-1

Library of Congress Cataloging-in-Publication Data

Stepanek, Mattie J. T. (Mattie Joseph Thaddeus)
    Just Peace : a message of hope / Mattie J.T. Stepanek with Jimmy Carter ; foreword
by Jimmy Carter ; edited by Jennifer Smith Stepanek.
        p. cm.
      ISBN-13: 978-0-7407-5712-9
      ISBN-10: 0-7407-5712-1
      1. Peace. 2. Hope. I. Carter, Jimmy, 1924- II. Stepanek, Jennifer Smith. III. Title.

JZ5538.S74 2006
303.6'6—dc22

Artwork by Mattie J.T. Stepanek: xx, 35, 156, 159, 175, 199
Artwork by Chris Dobbins: iii, 200; Cyril Huze: 198 bottom

All photos courtesy of Jeni Stepanek except where noted:
Ida Mae Astute/ABC: 7; Children's National Medical Center: 193; Children's Peace Pavilion: 132 top and bottom; Ralph Chite: 195 center; Christopher Cross: 43 center; CNN Larry King Live: 91; Devin Dressman: 38 top; Daniel Fromme: 197 bottom; Jim Hannah: 131 bottom; Harpo Productions: 128; Jim Hawkins: 47 top, 56 center, 152 top, 194 top; Shelly Heesacker: 30 bottom; Helen Hemelgarn: 42 top; Ralph Hirales: 197 center; Holy Rosary Catholic Church: 107 right; Nancy Hunt: 94 bottom; International Association of Fire Fighters: 70 bottom, 190 bottom, 191 top; Lynn Jones: 198 center; Paul Kammet: 197 top; Sally Lieberman: 93 center; Jimilu Mason: 195 bottom; Lyn Mox: 5; Katie McGuire: 38 center, 39 top; Patrick McMullen: 95 bottom right; Muscular Dystrophy Association: xix, 39 bottom, 40 top and bottom left, 43 bottom, 77, 99 right, 170, 176; Sandy Newcomb: 191 bottom, 194, 195 top; Bill O'Leary/Washington Post: 190 top; Rosalynn Carter Institute: xxii bottom right; Randy Sisulak: 33 center; Sal Tresca: 122 top left; Alvin Turner: 196; We Are Family Foundation: 92 bottom, 93 top and bottom, 95 bottom left; Yong Sung Lee Studios: 33 top

Please visit the following Web sites for more information about the authors and organizations featured in this book:
• www.mattieonline.org and/or www.mattieonline.com
• www.cartercenter.org
• www.mdausa.org
• www.wearefamilyfoundation.org
• www.kidpeace.org

ATTENTION: SCHOOLS AND BUSINESSES

We are each messengers,
called to bring hope and peace
to others, who then may choose
to become messengers for yet others,
for the world, and for the future.
This book is dedicated to children
and all other people who suffer
from an absence of hope and peace.
May this simple message
touch hearts and minds, spirits and lives,
and inspire each member of humanity
to make a gentle choice,
and become a messenger.

With love and respect,
Mattie and Jimmy

Contents

Acknowledgments

When Mattie asked me to edit and fulfill his plans for this book, I was honored that he entrusted me with something so important to him and that he had worked on with incredible devotion for so many years. As I began the arduous task of sifting through his papers after he died, I was awestruck by the multitude of pages filled with such remarkable insight and wisdom from a young man who lived to be barely a teenager. At the same time, I felt heartbroken by the empty reality that this young man, who was my youngest child, my best friend, my life, and my future as I knew it and hoped for it, had eternally passed from my mortal touch and being. Yet as I read his words and passages again and again in my effort to organize and complete the book according to his wishes, I realized that this project had become Mattie's gift to me—the gift of opportunity for realization, and a bit of rejuvenation for my aching spirit. While I was always intrigued by Mattie's concept of peace beginning with the choices each person makes in each moment, in integrating his message into this manuscript, I began to realize how he came to believe that peace is possible, and I recognized the truth of his convictions. Now, I know that peace truly begins with each of us somehow being "OK" with who we are as a person, even if life seems overly filled with burdens and losses.

Mattie lived with many daily challenges and much physical, emotional, and spiritual pain. But he was also blessed with the recognition that life is worthy, and with the realization that he, like everyone else in the world, has some reason to be here—some essential purpose that matters in some moment of time. And so, when we think of Mattie now, or when we hear his name, what we remember is his smile, his optimism, his strong spirit, and we feel good about life, and even about ourselves. When I consider the lessons I have learned in editing this book, I know in my heart and spirit that Mattie was blessed with this recognition and realization because so many other people took the time to let him know that he mattered, and that he was worthy of their energy, their support, their love. Therefore, in spite of all the stress and sadness, Mattie was OK with being "Mattie," and this allowed him to seek and find peace with others and with his world. And I know that even in my immense loneliness of loss, I am blessed with the same gifts of recognition and realization if I open my heart and spirit to them.

There is no simple yet thorough way to acknowledge the support and unconditional love we have received from our dear friend, Sandy Newcomb. Many people will recognize her name as that of "the e-mail update lady" or "our next door neighbor" or "Mattie's other-mother" or his "VFABF" (very favorite adult best friend). But the truth is that beyond any defining phrase, Sandy's generous spirit and untiring presence have been a welcome and much needed force and strengthening rock in our lives. Mattie and I have been blessed to have Sandy, and her children, as our kin—"Hedder" (Mattie's "other-other-mother" who spent long hours caring and advocating for him in the hospital and at home), "Jamie D." (Mattie's "rich and sweaty friend" who was always able and willing to help him "play after every storm"), Chris (Mattie's "kin-brother" who introduced Mattie to his first "Lego creation" way back in 1990 and who, as Mattie's new "book illustrator," designed the "Just Peace logo"), Cynthia (Mattie's "sister-in-law" who always had a smile and hug for him), and Kaylee (Mattie's little "niece" with whom he shared mutual adoration, and who lights up with an excited grin and "Mom-mom, there's Uncle Mattie!" whenever we look at his photographs or books or talk about him).

We have been blessed with close friends like Nell (friend of "Party Bear" and playful victim of Mattie's "duck on the head" practical joke) and Larry Paul (who still believes in "fried never-chicken"), Hope Wyatt (Mattie's best "kid friend" since kindergarten and who caught Mattie's adolescent eye when she wore "the green dress"), Diane Tresca (who has always brought us a message of hope, or at least laughter, when most needed), Mary Lou Smith (Mattie's "AML" who prays us through safe travels as we share hope and peace with others around the country), Devin Dressman (Mattie's MDA Summer

Camp counselor and year-round buddy and confidante), Madison Cross (who shared friendship and time with Mattie all the way from California), Sean Astin (aka "Samwise," who is following through on his promise to Mattie to keep the message of hope and peace spreading), and Laura Becker Gultekin (Mattie's primary home and hospital intensive care nurse, who always respected and treated Mattie as a person, not just a patient).

There are people and organizations that have helped us survive in some of our most difficult times, like Valerie Etherton, the Pfleigers, the Beaudets, the Retzlaffs, the Odens, the Moxes, and the Children's National Medical Center. There are people and organizations that have helped us celebrate in some of the best of times, like Billy Gilman, the Crosses, the Muscular Dystrophy Association, the We Are Family Foundation, the Children's Peace Pavilion, and the King Farm Community in Rockville, Maryland, as well as Andrews McMeel Publishing (especially Jean Lucas, Becca Schuler, and Jennifer Collet) and Hyperion/VSP Publishers. And there have been unique and treasured friendships with "real-life heroes," like Jimmy Carter, who supported Mattie at so many levels as he struggled to find peace for himself during his final year of life, and who truly believed in Mattie's endeavor to offer a lasting message of hope and "just peace" for the world through this book.

All of these people and groups and so many, many more have been messengers of hope and peace for Mattie, and for me. Because of them, Mattie and I have been able to be "OK" with who we are as people, and somehow balance the burdens and the blessings of our lives and find solace and meaning in so many moments. Since Mattie died, I have spent countless days and nights and mornings filled with grief and regrets, often wondering how I might ever find reason to get out of bed again. And for many, many days, the reason was to keep my promise to my son, and edit and fulfill his plans for this book. I now thank all the people—those I know in person, those who are famous, those who are known only in their own small circles of life, even those whom I have never met—for being a part of Mattie's spirit of hope and peace, which helped my son become the best person he could be on his journey through life. Although he is no longer here in body, my son continues to be my teacher. I know that some-how, even in my sorrow of not having Mattie and my first three children tangibly present, there can still be hope and peace for me, and for others, once we choose to embrace these realities. Mattie lived to be "almost four-teen" years old, but the gentle wisdom he has given us through his reflec-tions, his words, and his life are eternal gifts for each of us—if we choose to recognize and realize these lessons.

Preface

BY JENI STEPANEK (MATTIE'S MOM)

Hope is a garden
Of seeds sown with tears,
Planted with love
Amidst present fears.

Excerpt from "About Hope," May 21, 2003,
by Mattie J.T. Stepanek, in *Reflections of a Peacemaker:
A Portrait Through Heartsongs*
(Andrews McMeel Publishing, 2005)

Mattie J.T. Stepanek envisioned a world at peace. He believed that people are inherently good and generous, and that life is sacred and worthy of celebration. He was committed to making a positive difference in a world filled with conflict by gently reminding people about peaceful attitudes and habits that create a harmonious reality. And from a very early age, Mattie exemplified his personal philosophy that motivated him to cope with the many challenges of his own life, filled with disability and death and a desire for peace: "Remember to play after every storm."

Mattie was always thinking and planning, playing and pondering, and excitedly working on many projects that reflected his varied interests. He spent hours building new Lego creations, and hours scheming his next round of practical jokes. There were hours devoted to designing comic strips and characters, and hours recording his never-ending "Top Ten" lists in every category imaginable (including lists of "things to list"). Many hours passed negotiating with his health-care providers as he procrastinated over painful but necessary medical procedures, and many hours passed just sipping a cup of tea and enjoying a game of chess. But more than anything else, Mattie spent countless hours reading and writing and considering all the different ways he could share his message of hope and peace with the world.

Like many other children, Mattie was frequently asked, "What do you want to be when you grow up?" His response was not a typical one, though: "I want to be a peacemaker. . . . I want to serve as an ambassador for humanity through my thoughts and words and actions." And, like many other children who have life-threatening conditions that may prevent them from living long enough to "grow up," Mattie was asked on numerous occasions to share his "top three wishes." There are wonderful organizations that strive to grant at least one of three wishes for a child who is challenged by the reality of a shortened life span. Most children's wishes include trips to theme parks, shopping sprees, or meeting a favorite celebrity. Again, Mattie's "three wishes" response was not typical:

> I wish to have at least one of my collections of Heartsongs poetry published as my gift to the world. I wish to have Oprah Winfrey share the message of hope and peace in my Heartsongs on her show because people turn to her for inspiration and direction. And, I wish to have fifteen minutes to talk peace with Jimmy Carter so that I can make sure I am doing all that I can and should be doing to become a peacemaker for others.

During June 2001, when it became very clear that Mattie was edging closer to the probability of imminent death, the medical professionals at Children's National Medical Center in Washington, D.C., inquired about his wishes. Like others, they suggested "a computer" or other alternate wish-fulfillment ideas, because his three wishes were not considered "fantasy" or "practical" and, thus, did not fit the protocol of most wish-granting organizations. But Mattie never wavered from his goal of becoming a peacemaker, nor from his top three wishes of offering gifts to the world that would last beyond his mortality. His doctors were so moved by his sincerity that they asked the public relations office to at least explore the remote possibility that any one of Mattie's wishes could be granted.

Within days, a local family-run publishing company offered to reproduce one of Mattie's collections of Heartsongs poetry, and even stage a "mock booksigning" for him at the hospital. When they read through Mattie's materials, however, they made plans to offer him an actual contract for authentic publication of what they considered very creative and powerful poetry. Oprah Winfrey, who happened to be in the area that week, read an article in the local newspaper about Mattie and his wishes, and vowed to share his message on her show in the fall when her taping season resumed. And, Jimmy Carter telephoned the Pediatric Intensive Care Unit and spent fifteen minutes conversing with and answering the questions of a ten-year-old boy who was passionate about life and peace.

Throughout his "almost fourteen" years of life, Mattie composed thousands of poems, essays, and journal entries about the world as he saw it, filled with grief and growth, disaster and delight, compassion and catastrophe. He published six best-selling volumes of his poetry, and contributed passages or chapters to numerous writing projects of other people. He participated in hundreds of interviews for television, magazines, and newspapers, and he delivered dozens of speeches—about peace, about disability, about facing death, about celebrating life, about being an advocate, about education, about decision making, about spirituality—to politicians, to schoolchildren, to business leaders, to youth groups, to medical professionals, to university students—to any size group of any nature who gathered to listen to his inspirational message of hope. But the project that became Mattie's greatest passion was writing a book about the simple yet profound endeavor of planning peace.

In December 2001, Mattie had the honor and privilege of meeting his "real-life hero for peace," former President Jimmy Carter. The two met on the set of *Good Morning America*, as the hosts introduced the books each of them had recently published. Mattie was elated when he realized that he was really sitting next to his hero, and not a celebrity look-alike (which was his first thought when told that Jimmy Carter was in the studio). A day or so later, he and Jimmy began what would become an ongoing, and oftentimes intense personal friendship via phone calls, regular e-mail correspondence, and occasional opportunities to work together in person.

Through their Internet dialogues, Mattie and Jimmy swapped funny stories and kept each other informed of day-to-day happenings. They exchanged thoughts and insights on current events, and they chatted about lessons learned from personal experiences—some of them joyful and some of them painful. Mattie also shared his feelings on being a young teenager reckoning with his own early death, and Jimmy supported him through many emotional challenges as Mattie's body slowly died despite his strong and determined mind and spirit. And through their e-mails, they discussed the evolving plans for a book Mattie invited Jimmy to work on with him. Mattie was thrilled when Jimmy not only supported his notion of the venture, but also pledged to help make the project, as Mattie was planning it, a reality.

Mattie titled the book *Just Peace* because of the many connotations of the word *just*, especially as the various meanings complemented the multi-faceted concept of *peace*. In his journal, Mattie wrote:

> Either of the two words in this chosen title deserve considerate deliberation. "Just" can imply now, recently, lately, or very soon; it can imply only, solely, barely, exactly, entirely, or perfectly; it can also imply simply, really, truly, clearly, or specifically; or, it can imply impartial, honest, moral, honorable, truthful, fair, right, or equitable. "Peace" can imply calm, quiet, stillness, tranquility, or silence; it can imply harmony, serenity, concord, or amity; it can also imply understanding, reconciliation, agreement, compromise, synchronization, good will, or good relations; or, it can imply ceasefire, end of war, freedom from strife, or lack of violence. These are only a few of the many denotations and connotations and incredible power of the phrase "just peace."

The purpose of the book was to offer insights on why conflict and violence exist in a world filled with people who are generally and genuinely good, and to explore the potential impact and current justification of war in modern society. Most of all, Mattie wanted to share his thoughts on the "profound simplicity of choosing and planning peace, if it is deemed something that really matters in all aspects of thinking and speaking and being."

Some of the material for the book would come from an integration of Mattie's research, reflections, and recommendations about the situation of violence and war and the need for justice and peace. But a large part of the book was to be based on interviews Mattie would conduct with others who were endeavoring to seek peace and justice for individuals or groups of people around the world. The peacemakers Mattie hoped to include in this project would represent many different nations and many different concepts essential to a just peace, such as the equitable provision of basic needs to all people, the application of humanitarian laws in all places, and the security of human and civil rights across all cultures.

Mattie died before being able to complete his planned work for this book. Much of the last few years of his life were spent battling his neuromuscular disease in the hospital as his health steadily declined, though his love and optimism for people and life and the future never wavered. He spent his final six months of life literally struggling to breathe in the intensive care unit, but determined to go on "even a bit longer," and ever-dedicated to realizing his vision of *Just Peace*.

Because of the amount of time he spent in the hospital, and because of the many medical and physical complications from the progression of his neuromuscular disease, Mattie never had the opportunity to do any of the interviews that were to become the core of this book. However, because of his untiring allegiance to the possibility of peace, and the many hours, weeks, and months of work he had put forth in his efforts to study, plan, and create the vision for this book, Mattie laid the groundwork for the completion of this project. Mattie's body died on June 22, 2004, less than a month before his fourteenth birthday. While he never had the opportunity to grow old and fulfill an adult career aspiration, his spirit grew strong, and the gifts of his thoughts and words and actions will touch lives in many nations and across many generations. His message of hope lives on through the words he offered us in his journals, essays, poems, speeches, letters, notes . . . even in his lists of things that merited recording. And from his top three wishes, which were all generously fulfilled by so many people, came the opportunity for Mattie to become what he wanted to be when he grew up . . . an ambassador for humanity.

In the months after his death, I gathered, sorted, and compiled as much of Mattie's material as I could find related to this project. I was determined to fulfill my reassurance and my promise to my son during the hours before his death, that he had indeed been the best person he could be, that he had done everything a person could do to make a gentle and positive difference in life, and that he had completed enough of the work on this project that the book *Just Peace* would become a reality. Through it all, Jimmy Carter remained faithfully committed to the completion of this project as well, and he actively supported Mattie's request that the book be finished and published so that his message of hope could continue to touch the world.

While the project could not be completed in the way Mattie originally planned—integrating the insights and experiential lessons of peacemakers through a series of interviews—the book follows Mattie's original outline and addresses each goal he considered essential for planning a just peace. The manuscript is organized into three sections that explore Mattie's concept of the world and all people as a unique mosaic of gifts, the shattering of this mosaic due to ongoing violence and escalating destruction associated with war and injustice, and the rebuilding of the mosaic through the endeavor of planning peace.

Each section contains two essays from Mattie's work, related to thematic issues tackled in that section. The essays are woven together with other sources of communication from Mattie, including selections of his poetry about peace and portions of his e-mail correspondence with several individuals. Some of the e-mails are related to his advocacy work with organizations that support children and families, or from the transference of academic assignments to home or school teachers, or from his responses to catastrophic events in the world. Most of the e-mails, though, come from the many Internet conversations between Mattie and Jimmy Carter as these two peacemakers coped with life and hoped for the future through mutual support and goals.

And so, in the pages of this book, readers are offered Mattie's vision for a world at peace. Glimpses of Mattie's struggles to find peace on his personal journey through life are found in his autobiographical notes and communications. And there are formal passages presenting synthesized reflection and research, as Mattie shares his perceptions of and propositions for a world in conflict. But throughout each section of this book, Mattie's message is clear: Peace grows from the choices we each make, in our attitudes and in our habits, which become our reality now, and the echo of our essence in the future.

Sadly, Mattie is not physically here to witness the assemblage and presentation of his efforts. Joyously, though, Mattie never intended this book to be a personal achievement or even a culmination or completion of his endeavor to spread a message of hope and to nurture justice and peace. The project of *Just Peace* merely begins with this book; it continues through the ongoing commitment of individuals and organizations to make a positive difference, right here and throughout the world, right now and throughout the future. The endeavor now belongs to each of us, as we accept Mattie's simple gift and his profound challenge—to reflect and reason on the important matter of these issues, these thoughts, this message of hope, and the possibility of a just peace.

Two individuals who shared a strong spirit, mutual respect, admiration, and appreciation, and a desire for hope and peace for individuals and for the world, Jeni and Mattie Stepanek.

Just Peace

If I could change
One thing in this world,
It would be war.
Instead of war . . . peace.
But I especially don't want
World War Three,
Because we would
Blow up the earth.

If I could change
One thing in this world
We would have no weapons.
No knives or swords.
No guns or bombs.
Just peace.
Just peace.

By Mattie J.T. Stepanek, February 17, 1998,
in *Hope Through Heartsongs* (Hyperion/VSP, 2002)

Foreword

BY JIMMY CARTER

Peace has eluded mankind since the beginning of time. Entire institutions with multimillion-dollar budgets pay highly skilled negotiators to go out into the world for the purpose of peacemaking; government agencies are established for the peaceful resolution of issues that divide cities, states, and whole nations; we individuals spend much of our lives seeking inner peace. Still, turmoil, conflict, and war continue to afflict us.

So how could one small boy presume to reach such an unattainable goal? Since I have raised four precocious children of my own and enjoy a close relationship with eleven grandchildren who never cease to amaze me with their mature grasp of difficult concepts, I was not surprised by the notion. However, I was touched by the depth of passion and awed by the firm resolve with which Mattie Stepanek pursued a dream that has evaded men and women throughout history.

What began as a casual discourse, not too different from others I have had with inquisitive young people who have reached out to me, became a treasured and enlightening friendship that changed my life forever. With the purity of heart that only a child can possess, and the indomitable spirit of one who has survived more physical suffering than most adults will ever know, Mattie convinced me that his quest was not inconceivable. Inspired by his enthusiasm and without reservation, I committed to a partnership with him.

Though he was called to Heaven before completing the project as he had planned it, the message in Mattie's essays and correspondence is simple and clear. Listen to his Heartsong that reverberates throughout the pages that follow, learn to hear your own, and you, too, will be emboldened to take up the challenge of the ages: *Just Peace.*

These words of wisdom and inspiration came from the most remarkable person I have ever known.

Mattie and Jimmy share conversation and laughter during a dinner at the Kennedy Center, Washington D.C., October 2002. Later that evening, Mattie would introduce Jimmy and Rosalynn Carter for a televised speech.

Mattie with Jimmy and Rosalynn Carter at the Kennedy Center, Washington, D.C., October 2002.

Rosalynn Carter holds the "Carter Clock" made by Mattie with hourly reminders to be "playful, prayerful, and peaceful," July 2003.

Just Peace

The
Mosaic Vision

Hope is a rainbow
Of butterfly wings,
Gently it beckons,
Lightly it sings.

Excerpt from "About Hope," May 21, 2003,
by Mattie J.T. Stepanek, in *Reflections of a Peacemaker:
A Portrait Through Heartsongs*
(Andrews McMeel Publishing, 2005)

Hope Haiku

Gentle and peaceful . . .
We are the children of one God,
Yet, so many faiths.

True, we are different . . .
Unique mosaic of life.
Still, we are the same.

United, we are . . .
The festive fabric of life.
Divided, we fall.

By Mattie J.T. Stepanek, September 13, 2001,
in *Celebrate Through Heartsongs* (Hyperion/VSP, 2002)

Mattie dressed up for "Mardi Gras" during an MDA/IAFF Softball
Tournament, September 2003.

Mattie J.T. Stepanek's Journal, June 22, 2001

Summary of phone call from President Jimmy Carter to the
Pediatric ICU at Children's National Medical Center

MY THIRD WISH:
"FIFTEEN MINUTES WITH JIMMY CARTER
TO 'TALK PEACE'"

First, I thanked President Carter for calling me, and I told him that he's my hero and role model because he's a "humble peacemaker." He goes around the world helping people understand and want and plan peace, but then he doesn't go to the media and say, "Look what I've done." Instead, he says, "Look at what these people have done," or "Look at what this country has done." He goes to the media not to seek personal power or fame, but to make a difference because the media can be a powerful tool. He uses the recognition of his name and his essence to make a difference for others, and that is powerful and motivating to me. I told him that I want to be a peacemaker, too, through my writing and through public speaking. I want to be an ambassador for humanity.

I asked the following questions:
• What has been your most interesting experience as a peacemaker?
• What has been your most challenging peacekeeping effort?
• What is the most interesting place you have ever visited?
• Who is the most interesting person you have ever met?
• Who is your hero?
• What grade do you teach in Sunday School?
• What is your personal philosophy for life?

President Carter's answers included discussions of his peacekeeping efforts in the African countries of Sudan and Uganda during 2001, which were both the most challenging and the most interesting of his missions. We discussed the challenges and benefits of seeking and planning peace.

He listed Harry S. Truman as a hero. He said that he didn't teach "a grade" but rather a "group gathering" at his church in Georgia. We talked about the blessings of being able to teach others in a spiritual setting, and realized that we are doing similar things for other people of all ages, even though I am teaching the second graders rather than a general group of people who have gathered to listen and learn. President Carter said that his personal philosophy for life is: "If you want something bad enough, never give up trying for it and you will succeed." He told me that he liked my philosophy for life: "Remember to play after every storm." We agreed that sometimes, having a motto to take our spirit into the next moment is an important part of realizing peace for one's self, which is essential to finding and keeping peace with one's neighbor and one's world.

Finally, I thanked him, again, for calling me, and I asked him if he would like to read one of my Heartsong books, which are about peace for individuals and for the world.

I was so honored and excited to receive this phone call from my real-life hero for peace. And now, I will continue working toward my goal of being a peacemaker for all, through my poetry, and my essays, and my speeches, and my choices in how I live my life each day.

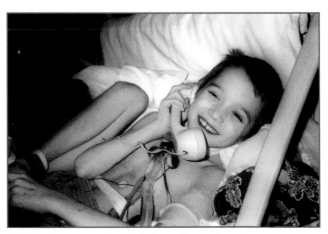

Mattie's first conversation with Jimmy Carter, June 2001.

E-mail from: Mattie J.T. Stepanek
Date: December 07, 2001 9:04 AM EST
To: Jimmy Carter
Subject: (no subject)

Dear Jimmy,

Thank you so very, very, VERY much for spending time with me on Tuesday. I can't believe that I met you! I can't believe that you cleared your schedule for me. I can't believe that I am one of your heroes. I don't feel like I am anybody but Mattie.

I kept saying to my mom all day "pinch me, I must be dreaming." We drove home from New York all night. And then the next morning my mom woke me up saying "Mattie, we're in New York. Wake up, honey. You have to go on *Good Morning America.*" I told her I just dreamed that I was already on the show and that you were with me, and that it was so wonderful and seemed so real. She said "tell me your dream later, it sounds great, but we're running late." I started crying because I was so sad that it was only a dream. Then she hugged me and said "I'm sorry, I was only kidding. It wasn't a dream, you really did meet him." It's funny now, but I didn't like the joke then.

I would be very sad if it had been a dream, because you matter so much to me. You make me really think about my life, and my world. Can I ask you a question? Is it hard for you to be famous and for everyone to know you everywhere you go? I love my message being famous, but I feel embarrassed when people act like I am famous. I feel like I am just Mattie, who is a messenger. God gives me the messages. I am just me. I want my message of hope and peace and Heartsongs to go around the world, and really make a difference. My mom told me to look to you again to learn, because you are humble. You must get very tired sometimes with everyone wanting to talk with you. But you are very gracious about it, she said. And she is right. You are my real hero in more ways than I thought before. I want to learn to be like you.

Mattie's first meeting with Jimmy Carter on the set of ABC's *Good Morning America,* December 2001.

Did you ever have hard times? I mean inside? Like you wondered about your message? My message is very real. I do believe in peace and hope and forgiving. But once in a while, I feel very stressed inside, and almost torn up. I am so upset about having a disability and knowing that for the rest of my life I will be on life-support, which means I won't be independent. I am upset knowing that I will probably die while I am a kid or teenager . . . I get upset knowing that I get scared about all these things. I still know I believe in peace, but I hurt inside. Then, someone will ask me to talk about peace, and I believe in my words, but sometimes, I wish I could feel them ALL the time, not just most of the time. Then, I feel guilty for not feeling peaceful inside, when I tell people how important it is. Am I still a peacemaker? Can I learn to be peaceful all the time? I am worried that I will not do a good job because even though I know and believe in peace, sometimes, it's in my mind and heart but a little distant from my spirit. How can I be better?

Love, Mattie

E-mail from: Jimmy Carter
Date: December 11, 2001 12:53 PM EST
To: Mattie J.T. Stepanek
Subject: (no subject)

Mattie: I'm in St. Louis, and finally got my e-mail hooked up. It was great to have your letter. I'm on a book tour re *Christmas in Plains*, and everywhere I go (New York, San Diego, Phoenix, Seattle, Denver, Atlanta, etc.) people are talking about our meeting on the *Good Morning America* program. Also, I've been signing a lot of your poetry books. It's truly amazing what an impact you have had on people, and as a peacemaker. When I taught my Bible class Sunday, the text was from Isaiah and referred to the Prince of Peace, and I emphasized that there are at least two kinds of peace. One is an absence of conflict, and the other is much more impor-tant—a sense of peace within the human heart. Your words and example provide this kind of peace.

When I sign books in a store (often as many as 2,000), the owner usually offers me a book to read on the way home. Last week, I chose Stephen Hawking's new one and read it, although there was a lot that I couldn't understand. He is, perhaps, the most brilliant and productive of all physicist/astronomers. I presume you already know about him. For many years he has been totally immobile, unable to speak—I think, with muscular dystrophy. His first book, *A Brief History of Time*, sold tens of millions of copies. I mention this to you so that you won't let your physical problems be a handicap or a source of excessive concern.

Mattie, all of us have deep inner problems. During my life there have been many times when I felt frustrated and doubted that I could fulfill a worthy destiny. Even Jesus had these feelings of unworthiness and abandonment. It may be that these are ways to build inner strength so that when real tests come along we will be able to meet them and prevail. You have been given a brilliant mind, and now a worldwide forum within which you can express your wisdom and insight to millions of people. One real test will be to retain two things: humility and truthfulness. I hope you will be able to relax, enjoy life, remain true to yourself, remember that you have friends who care about you, and let your Heartsongs be genuine. As you know, you are one of my heroes, and I have full confidence in you.

With love, Jimmy Carter

After six months of conversation by telephone and mail, Mattie and Jimmy share a heartfelt hug during a commercial break during their first in-person meeting on ABC's *Good Morning America*, December 2001. In November 2005, viewers nationwide voted this surprise visit their "number-one favorite event" in the thirty-year history of the program.

Jimmy signs Mattie's 2001 "Signature Book" on the set of *Good Morning America*. After meeting on the program and discussing their recent projects, Mattie suggested in an e-mail to Jimmy that they work together on a publication filled with poems and passages about peace. Later, they would agree to name this book *Just Peace*.

Unfolding

Born of the
Dust of humility,
Spread on the
Wings of pride,
Carried by
Winds of hope,
I grow with the
Ebbing life tide.

By Mattie J.T. Stepanek, January 1, 2001,
in *Loving Through Heartsongs*
(Hyperion/VSP, 2003)

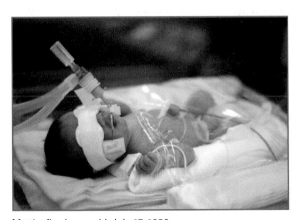

Mattie, five hours old, July 17, 1990.

JUST PEACE: AN INTRODUCTION

War is terrible. It leads to death, damage, and dismay. War is destructive. It devastates life, land, and culture. War is not necessary. It does not ever really "solve" any conflicts, situations, or problems. Even so, we, the people, choose to make war.

Headlines in the early twentieth century referred to World War I as the "war to end all wars." Yet, as we enter the early decades of the twenty-first century, it is clear that war has not ended. My own country has entered into war many times since then. We, the people, spend time judging whether we agree or disagree with the causes and matters of each war. We discuss which war has been "the worst" based on statistics measuring the losses—economic, property, and human. Sometimes, we even contemplate the possibility of a world without war. We study peace, stage demonstrations protesting violence, and vow to attempt mediation before annihilation. But still, the rages and wages of war are witnessed worldwide.

I do not understand how, or why, the terrible, destructive, and unnecessary confusion of war remains such a strong and evident reality. I fear that the clutches of a third world war will grab what is left of humanity and Earth. We, the people, are intelligent and compassionate and creative in seeking solutions. We realize that the strategies and efforts of making war are time-consuming, expensive, and controversial. Perhaps if we choose to invest as much time and energy in planning and making peace as we have spent in planning and making war, we could be at a different point in history.

It is my hope and prayer, and my mission, to share a message of peace—just peace—with the world. Peace is possible. It can begin simply, over a game of chess and a cup of tea. I believe that peace becomes possible when we choose to make peace an attitude and a habit. I believe that the reality of peace begins within each one of us, when we have our basic needs met and when we are satisfied with who we are as a person; peace continues through our understanding, interactions, and involvement within and between our kin, our communities, and our countries; and peace is fulfilled through our respect of the earth and life, including ourselves and each other. I believe that we have, we are, a mosaic of gifts, to nurture, to offer, to accept. I believe that we need to think gently, speak gently, and live gently. I believe that we each have a unique song in our heart that is meant to be united in harmony with the unique song that grows in each and every other heart. I believe that we need to solve conflicts, situations, and problems with words and mutual collaboration, rather than with bombs and conquering invasion.

I believe that peace is just, and that peace is worthy, and that a plan for peace is more practical and achievable than we, the people, may realize. I believe that peace is possible for all people around the world, if we choose to make it something that really matters. And so, in this collection of thoughts gathered from my essays, poetry, speeches, letters, and conversations across the years, I offer you my message, and my hope and prayers, on the important and essential matter of peace—Just Peace.

Mattie sharing a smile and his hope for peace, May 2002.

December Prayer

No matter who you are,
Say a prayer this season.
No matter what your faith,
Say a prayer this season.
No matter how you celebrate,
Say a prayer this season.
There are so many ways
To celebrate faiths,
There are so many faiths
To celebrate life.
No matter who,
No matter what,
No matter how . . .
You pray.
Let's say a prayer
This season,
Together, for peace.

By Mattie J.T. Stepanek, December 1, 1999,
in *Journey Through Heartsongs*
(Hyperion/VSP, 2002)

"Angel Mattie," December 1994.

E-mail from: Mattie J.T. Stepanek
Date: December 19, 2001 9:46 PM EST
To: Jimmy Carter
Subject: (no subject)

Dear Jimmy,

Thank you for answering my letter. It really helped a lot. I sometimes feel a bit ashamed that I get anxious or depressed or angry. I tell other people about finding inner peace. And I believe in it, but sometimes there are just so many scary things in my life that it's hard to feel it. But I know what I do about my feelings is a choice. So, I will remember my Heartsong, and you, my hero. There are some storms going on right now . . . like the sore on the back of my head not healing and getting danger-ous . . . and like some financial and legal problems my mom and I are having. But things will be OK and I will keep praying, and then I will play after these storms.

Did you get the Christmas presents that I made for you? I hope you like them. They are for your wife to enjoy, too. And I hope you like the videotape that I made of your life. I think I was seven or eight years old when I made it. It was so much fun, except that I for-got to put shoes on when I was "president." I was still barefoot, like the "peanut farmer." My mom said that you probably wanted to be barefoot sometimes in the White House.

I really want you to know what a difference you have made in my life. You have been my hero for so many years, and you are so real. So real. I can handle things because I know that you are very real. You are not just in a book. You touch people, and life, and the future. And I thank you so much. I will try to touch people, and life, and the future in some of the same ways that you do.

I love you a lot. Merry Christmas, and thank you for being you.

Love, Mattie

E-mail from: Jimmy Carter
Date: December 20, 2001 12:03 PM EST
To: Mattie J.T. Stepanek
Subject: (no subject)

To Mattie: We received the great Christmas presents, and Rosalynn and I are very grateful. The miniature lamp is especially precious, with the painted shade and your personal inscription. The video is something I will have forever, and we appreciate your poems as do the thousands of other admirers. I'll be praying for the healing of the sore on your head . . .

With love, and best wishes for the holiday season, Jimmy Carter

E-mail from: Jimmy Carter
Date: December 20, 2001 10:30 PM EST
To: Mattie J.T. Stepanek
Subject: (no subject)

Mattie: Last night, after my wife, Rosalynn, came home from Atlanta, we watched your video together. We both laughed and cried together, with joy, just realizing how great it is to have you as a special friend. When my children and grandchildren arrive here in Plains for Christmas, we will see the video again—all twenty-one of us. By the way, tell your mother that she also did a great job as the interviewer.

While I'm at home for a few days, I'm kind of in charge of a special project in Plains, to renovate three buildings on our main street. (We only have eight in all.) I used to work in all three of them when I was a boy, to sell hamburgers and ice cream in one and to help my Uncle Buddy in his mercantile store. We will have an antique mall and an inn with seven rooms, so visitors will have a place to stay when they visit our town. I hope that some day you'll have a chance to do so.

Please stay in touch with me. Love, Jimmy

E-mail from: Mattie J.T. Stepanek
Date: December 22, 2001 9:23 AM EST
To: Jimmy Carter
Subject: (no subject)

Dear Jimmy,

I am so excited that you like the video. I loved making it. Please tell your family I didn't mean to forget shoes when you were president. My favorite part was at the end, when I talk about how you and I are alike in many ways. My mom likes the peanuts on the "The End" sign. I hope everyone in your family has a great Christmas "in Plains." (By the way, your book is rated higher than mine on many of the lists, and I am very happy about that. Maybe we should do a book together, and it would be number ONE!)

I would love to come visit sometime. My mom has promised me that she will take me to the Carter Center sometime, and to Plains to see where you learned about life and being you. My mom and I will say a prayer for your family and for the world on Christmas. We are just staying home that day. We go to Midnight Mass, and I sign "Silent Night" while the choir sings it during the meditation every year. Usually we go to the cemetery to see my brothers and sister on Christmas but this year we will go on Christmas Eve and the two of us will stay home and be a family alone but together on Christmas. I really want to just stay home and *be* on Christmas.

I almost didn't have this Christmas so it is very special. I love you very much. You are a hero, AND a friend, and the world is lucky you came along. Please tell Mrs. Carter I said hello, and Amy, and your family, and your grandchildren (especially the one who pretended like the little guy fell in the river in Africa and scared the mom! That was a funny joke!).

Love, Mattie

E-mail from: Mattie J.T. Stepanek
Date: December 25, 2001 11:23 AM EST
To: Jimmy Carter
Subject: (no subject)

Dear Jimmy,
  My best Christmas present of the day was your phone call! I love you and you love me. Life is good.

Love, Mattie

Mattie, Christmas morning, 2001, with another favorite gift, a book about peace given to him by his friend Oprah Winfrey.

Resolution Blessing

Let our breath be gentle wind,
Let our ears be of those who listen,
Let our hearts be not ones
That rage so quickly and
Thus blow dramatically,
And uselessly.
Let our spirits attend and be
Most diligent to the soft
Yet desperate whisper of
Hope and peace for our world.
Let our souls be those
Which watch for the Lord,
Waiting with wonder and want.
Let our eyes be attentive
With interest and respect,
Let our minds be committed
To health and happiness,
Let our hands join
In helpful resolution
To being our best person,
Praying and playing and
Passing through moments
Of pain or memory-
Makers of pleasure
Touching the future, together.

By Mattie J.T. Stepanek, January 1, 2003,
in *Reflections of a Peacemaker: A Portrait Through Heartsongs*
(Andrews McMeel Publishing, 2005)

A MESSENGER OF HOPE

Hello everyone, and welcome to these thoughts. I'd like to begin by sharing a few things about myself as a person, because then you may better understand my message of hope and peace.

MY BEGINNING

My name is Matthew Joseph Thaddeus Stepanek, but everyone knows me as "Mattie." I am the youngest of four children. My sister, Katie, was born in 1985. My oldest brother, Stevie, was born in 1987. My other brother, Jamie, was born in 1989. And I was born on July 17, 1990. Jamie and I were best friends for a while. But I didn't ever get to meet Katie and Stevie, because they died before I was born. And now, I don't get to see or be with Jamie anymore, because he died when we were both little boys.

All four of us were born with a rare neuromuscular disease called dysautonomic mitochondrial myopathy. It is one of the forty-three types of diseases that the Muscular Dystrophy Association (MDA) focuses on for support and research. Our particular form is very life threatening. From the time you are diagnosed with it, you know, or your family knows, that you probably won't live too many more years. Some people ask, "Why on earth did your mother have four kids who would inherit this terrible disease?" Well, the simple answer to that is my mom didn't know she was going to have babies with this life-threatening condition when she gave birth to us.

When my mom got married and began having babies, she could walk and run, and work and play like any other healthy person. She had the four of us in less than five years, and did not know that she would be diagnosed with the adult-onset form of the disease until after we were all born. Her four children were diagnosed with the deadlier childhood form of the disease after she was diagnosed. Back in the 1980s, when she first started having us, there wasn't a lot of information about mitochondrial myopathies. In fact, most doctors didn't even know to test for it when a baby was very sick and didn't fit the description of any other illness. So, my mom had her first three babies thinking that they all had a very good chance of being healthy. I was what she called a "welcome, but unplanned baby." Now, she tells people that I was a "spirit meant to be" because I have defied so many medical and developmental odds.

Before my mom was diagnosed in 1992, it was clear something was very wrong with her babies, but the doctors could only list our symptoms. We tested negative for everything they looked for medically. When the doctors learned that my mom had the adult-onset of this disease, that's when they began to realize what Jamie and I really had. Katie and Stevie had already died by then, but the doctors were able to look back at their medical records and confirm that they had this disease as well. My brother, Jamie, died during the next year, and in 1994, my mom began using a wheelchair to get around. Now she has to use it all the time because she is getting weaker every year. And I have gone through a lot of medical problems as well. It seems like every year, I get a little worse, and a little worse, and a little worse.

Dysautonomic mitochondrial myopathy is a very unusual neuromuscular disease. For my mom, who was diagnosed as an adult, it's mostly muscular. Her arms and legs are getting weaker and weaker, and so is her neck and jaw and back. It will shorten her life span some, but not as much as if you are diagnosed with it as an infant. For children who are born with this disease, it is devastating neurologically, and it hurts them muscularly, too.

What this disease does neurologically is that it causes the autonomic system, or automatic system, to malfunction. So, sometimes, my body and brain will do automatic things. But oftentimes, my body and brain don't remember to do automatic things, like breathing when I am awake and asleep, and keeping my heart beating the right way and at the right speed, and keeping my blood pressure at a healthy number that's not too high or too low. Everyone gets hot or cold depending on the weather and physical activity, but once my body gets hot or cold, it doesn't always remember how to adjust itself to get back to a normal temperature. Sometimes, my body has a hard time digesting certain foods, especially foods that have lots of fat or sugar.

One of the worst things that this disease does to me is that my body doesn't process oxygen correctly. So even when I look healthy and have pink lips and fingernails, my body doesn't always use the oxygen in my arteries, so my brain feels like it is suffocating. Then, my brain gets mixed up and sends bad messages to my automatic systems, and my body begins to go into a crisis, and things just get worse and worse from there. And the more times this happens, the weaker my body and systems get. As I get older and older, my spirit and mind get stronger and wiser, but my body and systems get weaker and more unstable trying to recover from all these dysautonomic storms.

MY LIFE

When I was born in 1990, the doctors didn't think I would live long. They also told my mom that if I did live, even for a bit, that there was a strong possibility that I would never be able to walk, talk, or think like a "normal child." Most of the doctors didn't think that I would live from year to year, because I was so sick and they didn't understand my disease well. But I lived to be one, then two, then five, then ten . . . and I keep living each year even though there are so many times that my body almost dies.

Even though I surprised people by surviving, I was very sick as a baby. I had a tracheostomy tube surgically inserted through my neck and into my trachea. The trach tube was then hooked up to a ventilator that breathed for me. I always had to use a lot of extra oxygen, I had a tube in my chest that went into my heart for all the blood transfusions and intravenous fluids I needed, and I had a tube in my nose for food because I was too weak to drink from a bottle.

When I was a toddler, I seemed to start doing better medically, so my mom and a doctor decided that we could take the trach tube out of my neck. Some of the doctors agreed, and some disagreed with the decision. But I am so happy that my mom agreed with the decision, because I had such an opportunity to do things in life for many years that I couldn't do if I was on all of the medical equipment that I had as a baby. For almost six years, I only had oxygen through a nasal canula, and monitors that alarmed when I would forget to breathe or when my heart rate wasn't right. It was great. During those years I learned to swim and dive, I body surfed in the ocean, I climbed hills and trees and rocks, and I earned my First Degree Black Belt in a form of martial arts that teaches self-control and respect for all people and life and earth. I also made lots and lots of friends in many different places while traveling with my mom, and I got to spend a few years going to my local public school before I began to get sicker again.

When I was a preschooler, many professionals were still concerned that even though I had survived, I may not be able to think and learn easily because of all the medical crises I lived through. When my mom first told people that I could read at age three, they were skeptical. Even she was surprised about it, because she never really taught me to read. She just tried to help me learn to speak clearly since my speech was very slurred and hard to understand. What she didn't realize is that I was accidentally learning the letters and phonics that were on the picture flash cards she was using to help me. By age four, I was beginning to read chapter books, and I was also beginning to write my own poetry and prayers and passages for books.

Lots of people ask me or my mom if I have ever been tested to determine my "IQ." Different professionals and systems have tested me across the years, and I am definitely very smart. But my mom has taught me that numbers on paper don't give all the information needed about people to understand how they think and learn, or what they have been exposed to so far in life, or what they choose to do with their gift of life. So, I know that I have an IQ score, but I do not know what it is, and I agree with my mom that it is not necessary for me, or anyone, to dwell on numbers.

I also know that I loved going to school. I ended up skipping some grades because everyone agreed that it would be good for me to have more challenging subjects and materials. I was very excited about learning things and being with people. But when I was eight, my body started having more and more medical problems. I could feel that my body was getting a little weaker and I knew that I was having more and more spells of dysautonomia that were getting worse. I needed to use more and more oxygen, and I was having a harder time keeping my energy up.

When I was almost nine years old, I began using a power wheelchair to help me conserve energy. I could still stand and walk, but I got tired so quickly, and using the chair helped me out a lot. I began homeschooling during the fall of 1999, because even with the wheelchair, it was getting harder and harder to have energy. It seemed like the more I did physically, the more dysautonomia symptoms I had. The good news is that as much as I loved going to school, I loved school at home just as much. I was able to begin taking high school courses, and I got to go to a community college a few hours a week for things like foreign language and government. I could get my work done quickly so that I had time to write poetry and play, and just relax with my mom. And on days that I was having a hard time medically, I didn't fall behind because I was the only one in my class, and I was already taking high school courses.

When I was almost ten years old, even with the easier schedule at home I had to start using a bipap machine at night to help me keep breathing. Then, I needed the machine to help me breathe during many hours of the day as well, and I was still getting sicker and sicker. The skin on my fingers and lips and feet began bleeding and eroding because my body could not process enough oxygen. My blood pressure and other vital systems and organs became unstable as my body and autonomic system began rapidly failing.

Early in 2001, I ended up in the intensive care unit for about five months. The doctors had to put the tracheostomy tube back into my neck, and I began using the ventilator that completely breathed for me like when I was a baby. I was in and out of comas, and many doctors didn't think I would live to be eleven years old. But again, I surprised doctors and friends. I lived, and I loved living. I told my mom that I didn't know how much time I had left on earth, but that I had decided to spend every bit of that time living until death happened, rather than dying until death happened.

Now, I am thirteen years old. A teenager. Something I thought would only be a dream, but it is a reality. Even during the last few days before my thirteenth birthday, I was so worried that something was going to happen and that I would not succeed in my desire to become a teenager. I have known for a while that I am "living on borrowed time." And although I have figured out that borrowed time ticks one second at a time just like regular time, somehow, those seconds seem to come a little closer together and each one is incredibly precious and appreciated.

The prognosis for my future is uncertain. I am in what professionals call "uncharted waters." No child diagnosed with this disease during infancy has ever lived this long. Some say I am lucky to live each day. Some say if every-thing is "perfect" I could maybe live many more years. And, some say that the hormonal and chemical changes that occur in the body during adoles-cence, which is beginning now, could cause such severe dysautonomia that my body will be unable to survive. My primary specialist, who is the most optimistic of all the doctors, has said it like this: "I wouldn't be surprised to hear at any time, 'Mattie died today.' But I'm not expecting it if we can stay at least two steps ahead of him medically."

MY REALITY

This all sounds very scary, right? Well, I have to be honest and tell you that it is very scary. When I think about my life story, I realize I spend a lot of time "almost" dying. It is the truth . . . I live on the edge. Sometimes I am closer to the edge than other times, but I am always on the edge. Since the day I was born, all the people in my life have known that I "might" die. And on some days, that reality is a mere possibility, and on other days, that real-ity seems more like a strong probability. There are days that I look or feel good, and there are days that I look or feel rotten. But each day is another day, and I feel blessed and joyfully thankful that I am here, even amid the challenges and pain.

I am not looking forward to death, because I love life on earth so much. I love people and I love nature, and I love being with my mom and I love being alive, even during the times that are so tough or painful that I com-plain. Like anybody else, I've asked the question, "Why me?" But then I think, or pray, or talk, and realize, "Why not me? Better me than a little baby who cannot understand what is happening. Better me than someone who already has just too much stress on his or her life." As much as I would like to not be the one living the challenges of my life, I cannot think of anyone else that I would give them to.

I believe that there is something bigger and better than the here and now where our essence, our spirit, lives eternally. And, I believe that I am spending my time on earth trying to do what I feel is my purpose here. I am trying to be the best me that I can be. And in doing so, I believe that the eternal wonders and glory of what I call "Heaven" will greet me when my body finally stops working. So, while I have to admit that I am afraid of the process of dying, I am not afraid of being dead.

When you hear my story, it may sound very sad. And in some ways, it is. I live alone with my mom, who is divorced and who cannot get around at all without her wheelchair. We spent many years living in the basements of other people's houses because we were financially poor and needed a place with no stairs because of our wheelchairs. I have three wonderful siblings, but they have all died from the same disease that I am dealing with, and that I will die from as well. I don't know from day to day what will happen to me medically. I do know that I will probably not grow old, and I will probably not even live long enough to drive a car, or to attend graduate school, or to become a daddy, which is one of my greatest desires.

Yes, my story is, in many ways, very sad. And angering. And scary. And frustrating. But I don't live sad, or angry, or scared, or frustrated. Of course I have all of these feelings in my life. But, I choose to do things to help me cope with these difficult feelings so that I can embrace the joy of living each day. I have experienced the worst of the worst at times, but I have also experienced the best of the best. I have felt the pain of loss and death and the anxious fear of living in medical unknowns. I have also had opportunities in life that others only dream of . . . meeting my real-life heroes, publishing my books, traveling and sharing my message of hope and peace with the world. What I try to do, though, is to live somewhere in the balance of the middle. I choose to "see my glass as half full, not half empty." I am alive, and I believe that I am here for a reason. I believe that every person on earth is here for a reason. And, I treasure that in spite of all the difficult things I have to cope with, I am just an ordinary kid blessed with the extraordinary gift of daily life.

COPING THROUGH APPRECIATION

Recognizing and respecting the value in "ordinary" is one of the things that helps me cope. What is ordinary about my life? I have good days and bad days. I have favorite things and things I dread. I have time that I spend alone and time that's just with me and my mom, and I have time that I spend giving and doing with others. In the midst of a life filled with things that don't always seem normal, I realize that normal and ordinary is a point of view measured by our own desires. And, I have learned to appreciate life as it happens, even with the ups and the downs and the days filled with the routine and the days filled with the extraordinary.

I love being "daddy" to my golden retriever, Micah. He's our service dog and he helps my mom and me with lots of different tasks. But he's so cute and he loves it when I give him belly rubs, and I love it when he hides my socks and when he jumps up in my bed and sleeps with me. I have favorite subjects in school, like social studies and literature. And, even though I do well in algebra and science, I repeatedly question why I need those least favorite subjects when my career goal is to be an ambassador of humanity through public speaking and writing.

In my free time, I create and build with Legos, I play video games and watch television or movies, and I enjoy spending lots of time on the phone or on the computer. I read everything I can find to read—best-sellers, classics, biographies, inspirations, the Bible, poetry, newspapers, magazines, comic books, even cereal boxes. I am well-known for my practical jokes (especially my remote-control fart machine and my mouse-in-the-box trick). I look forward to MDA Summer Camp each June, and I get excited about journaling during vacations. I also like to collect stuff . . . all kinds of stuff. I collect rocks, shells, trading cards, mementos, memories, even people and friends, everyplace I go, whether it's down the street or across the country. My mom says that slowly but surely, I am moving the whole world, piece by piece, right into my bedroom. When I look at all my treasures organized on the shelves, I know she is correct, and it makes me smile.

For community service, I teach some of the Sunday school classes and serve as a Minister of the Word in my church. Most recently, I got to work with the sixth grade class. But, my first (and favorite) experience was teaching the second graders ("my babies") about God and Heaven and love and mercy and grace. I also serve as the National Goodwill Ambassador for the Muscular Dystrophy Association, helping people understand about life with a neuromuscular disease, and how we can all be a part of bringing help and hope to children and families affected by these diseases. And, I love to travel and give speeches to people of all ages and backgrounds and futures so that they better understand the gift of life and Heartsongs and the importance of world hope and peace.

COPING THROUGH TALKING AND BELIEVING

Another thing that helps me cope with the challenges in my life is talking and interacting. When I say talking, I don't just mean public speaking. I like to talk "with" people, not just "to" people. I like learning about people. I believe that it is important to have role models, and heroes, and goals in life. I believe that even though we cheer for television and movie heroes, we should also learn about and cheer for and imitate the real-life people who do things, big things and small things, to make life a little better for the world in some way. And the more I learn, the more I know and understand, and, therefore, I am able to appreciate people and life even more.

One of the best people I can talk with is my mom. I have kid friends and adult friends, but my mom is my very best friend in the whole world. She has given me the gift of life so many times and she has taught me to appreciate it even more times. I have heard my mom say that she is my "greatest critic" and my "greatest fan." That is correct. My mom has taught me about humble pride, and she has taught me about things that really matter in life. My mom has taught me about reading and writing and history, and she has taught me about respect and character and touching life gently with our thoughts and words and actions. My mom has taught me that the world does not revolve around me or around anyone in particular, but she has also taught me that I, like everyone else, am an essential part of the revolving world. Having someone that you trust to listen and share and grow with is so important.

I also spend a lot of time talking with God. Talking with God is a lot like praying, but it involves listening with my heart and spirit and life to the inspiration of responses, rather than just saying or thinking things. Spirituality is a huge part of my life, and it is essential to my coping. I was baptized into the Roman Catholic Church when I was a baby, and was raised practicing all of the rituals of this religion. I chose to study for and make my Confirmation in this religion in 1999. And while I am proud to be a member of this church, I believe that religion and spirituality are two very separate, though related and essential, issues that are connected by faith.

A person can be very religious, yet not spiritual. And I know some very spiritual people who do not practice a particular religion. The way I have come to understand it, religion is much like a structural framework for spirituality. Religion is a set of beliefs and practices common to a group of people. Religion is filled with rituals that can make the joyful times even more celebrated, and that can help us get through the most difficult and painful things that happen in life. Spirituality is more personal. Spirituality is not defined by traditions and customs, but by a sense of purpose and being that somehow transcends our mortal understanding of time and space. Both religion and spirituality can help us make sense of things that are beyond our understanding. And, both religion and spirituality rely on faith.

Faith is acceptance, and faith is a gift. Faith is believing in something even if we cannot fully understand it, or prove it. As humans, we want proof of things. We want scientific knowledge and research and evidence. But there are some things that just cannot be fully understood or proven. And I believe that there are many ways to make sense of this reality, through various religions and through spirituality. I have chosen a religion that helps me to make sense of things, and that inspires me to find ways to cope with things that seem too hard to accept. I have faith in my religion and in my spirituality. I also accept and respect that others have faith in other beliefs and rituals that give strength to their spirits. Most of all, I believe that our spirituality should unite us in faith for our future, even though our religious tenets and traditions may be different. Sadly, this is too often not the reality, and religion becomes the root of conflict, rather than coping.

COPING THROUGH WRITING AND SHARING

One of the things that I do most often that has helped me cope with the reality of my life since I was very young is writing. I love to write. Writing is a creative way to express thoughts, experiences, and feelings. Writing to me is like running to an athlete. It's energizing and exercising, and it's healing and helpful to me, and sometimes to others as well. I write journal entries and essays. I write poetry and prayers. I write short stories and chapter books. I even write lists . . . lists of my goals, of my favorite things, of things to write about in the future.

I first realized my love and appreciation for writing and creating when I was three years old. My brother, Jamie, had recently died, and I was very sad and lonely without him. I knew that Jamie was "dead" but I didn't understand what "being dead" really meant. I was just aware of the fact that my brother, whom I loved dearly, was no longer in his bed, or his wheelchair, or my life. My mom tried to help me cope with my grief and feelings during this time. She taught me the words for all of the different feelings I had. She taught me ways to express my feelings in a manner that helped me feel better, but also did not hurt other people or things. And, she taught me that even though there are very sad experiences and times in life, there are also other times that can be filled with happiness and celebration if we choose to accept them.

As time passed, I began to play games that helped me process all the feelings I had about my brother's death. I was also dealing with changes in my own health, and in my mom's physical abilities. Being an "only child" of sorts, I played a lot of imagination games, and often played them out loud. Just as my mom had taught me about feelings and coping and living, I spent a good deal of playtime teaching my stuffed animals and Lego creations these same lessons. My animals would be angry or sad or scared or frustrated, and I would create plays with them or talk with them to help them feel better.

During many of these playtimes, my mother was in the same room doing her work. It wasn't unusual for me to see her sitting there writing while I was busy playing, because she only went to her office a couple of days a week, and did the rest of her work from home. One day, after helping one of Jamie's stuffed animals deal with some very sad and lonely thoughts, I went and sat by my mom on the couch. She had been writing off and on the whole time I was playing. I looked at her paper and began to sound out some of the words she had written, and then realized that what she had written down was my conversation with the stuffed animal.

"Why are you writing down what I am saying?" I asked her. She explained to me that part of what she did at work was help families who have children with disabilities cope with different feelings. She said that there wasn't a lot of information about how little children deal with some feelings, especially the sad feelings that happen when someone they love dies. She asked me if it was OK for her to share my thoughts and words with other people, to help them understand how little children cope and grow. I told her that I really liked the idea of helping other people, and of other people hearing "Jamie stories."

Then, she read back to me what she had written. I told her that it sounded a lot like the poems and meditations that we read together before bed each night . . . that the words start in the beginning or middle of some feeling or place, and take you to some other feeling or place by the end. And that is when I first began to understand that poetry is thoughts and feelings chosen into words, combined with sound and spacing chosen onto paper. I was fascinated by the process of creatively working with words in a way that helped me feel better, and that could also help other people. Within a few weeks, I was excitedly expressing my thoughts and feelings using all of my senses, my spirit, new words I was learning, and even new words I was making up to fit an idea.

I began asking my mom to write things down for me as I created poetry by the mouthful and the dayful. I also began using a tape recorder to capture my thoughts. By the time I was four years old, I was beginning to try to write my own poetry and passages. I laugh now when I see my large block-style printing as I proudly captured my own early expressions. And I am very happy that I eventually learned to write faster and smaller, and then type my words and expressions onto the computer.

MY MESSAGE AND MISSION

When I first began creating poetry and short stories as a preschooler, the content was mostly about my brother Jamie, and my feelings related to loss and grief. But as I grew, my poetry grew, too, evolving into other topics and messages. I have written a lot about nature, about senses, about friendships, about seasons, about disability, and about the challenges and joys of every-day life. I have also written a lot about spirituality, and about hope and peace. All of my writing, from that first day to this one, comes from my experiences and perceptions in life. Sometimes, I write from something I experience personally. Sometimes I react to something I have seen or read or heard about. And sometimes, I feel something deep inside of me that I just want to share with others. Most often, this is a message of hope and peace.

I have been calling my poetry collections "Heartsongs" since I was five years old. That name came to me one day when I was sharing a poem I had written about my happiness. I happened to be wearing a sweatshirt that had a little music maker sewn inside the front of it. As I leaned across the table sharing my creation with my mom, the music maker was activated, and the simple and sweet melody came out through my left chest area. I stopped and listened for a moment, and then said, "Mommy, listen! That's my Heartsong!" Across the years, I have shared my thoughts and description of what I believe is the essence of a Heartsong. I now have many volumes of my Heartsongs poetry collections published, and I am excited that they have all been best-sellers. I am excited about that because it means that people want to hear and learn about the important matter of Heartsongs.

A Heartsong is an inner message. It is a person's inner beauty and reason for being. A Heartsong tells you what you are meant to do, or be, in life. Whatever it is that we feel we need and want the most in life, well, that is what we are called to offer others. That is our Heartsong. I seek hope and peace. I seek happiness. I seek love around the world. So, most of the time, my Heartsong sings, "I love you! I love you! How happy you can be! How happy you can make this whole world be!" But sometimes, it sings different words and tunes, and that is OK, because it's always the same message.

I believe that everybody in the world has their own special Heartsong. No two Heartsongs are exactly alike, because they represent our spirit, our essence. That's good, though, because I believe that all of humanity is a mosaic of gifts. We each bring something unique and essential to the fabric of life. No single Heartsong is better, or more important, or more worthy, than any other Heartsong. And the beauty of Heartsongs is when they are realized, and shared with others. Like a worldwide chorus or symphony, we can each share our Heartsong in harmony with the Heartsongs of others. To do this, we must truly listen to our special song, and also listen to the special song that grows from the hearts of others. We must accept, and respect, and appreciate the unique differences for the unity of the mosaic of life.

Sometimes, people forget their Heartsongs, by choice or by life. Perhaps life has been so busy that someone forgets to take time to hear their special message. Perhaps life has been so filled with sadness or pain or anger or fear that someone does not remember that they have a beautiful message inside. Or, perhaps life has been so filled with joy and celebration and success that someone does not choose to continue following the message of their Heartsong. It is OK for people to borrow and share Heartsongs, though. If someone, especially an adult, cannot remember or recognize their song, they can always tune into someone else's Heartsong, especially that of a child. We should always be generous with sharing our Heartsongs. In borrowing and sharing, forgotten and unrealized Heartsongs are reawakened, and then they too become available for borrowing and sharing.

As we consider and follow and share our Heartsongs, we should also consider, while we are alive, how we would like the world to remember us, and our Heartsong, after we die. When people think of me, or hear my name once I have passed on, I hope they say things like, "Oh, yes, Mattie! He was a poet, a peacemaker, and a philosopher who played." I would like people to remember that I shared ideas like, "Follow your Heartsong!" and "Always remember to play after every storm." My mother taught me that how we reach out and touch the world in each moment is how the world will reach back and touch us in some other moment. And I believe that such an interaction, whether it is with one or many or millions, is how we will be remembered in the future.

So what is my reason for being? I believe that I am here to remind people about the gifts and value of Heartsongs and mosaics. I believe that I am here to share a message of hope and peace with the world. I believe that I am here to reach out and touch the world gently with my thoughts and my experiences, and with my observations and my reactions, to help people more fully appreciate and respect all aspects of life. I believe that I am here, even if only for a few handfuls of years, to help people consider the important matter of future, during our lifetime, and for eternity.

Mattie enjoying a day at the beach, summer 1995.

Mattie working on his computer, October 2001.

About Things That Matter

It matters that the world knows . . .
We must celebrate the gift of life
Every day in some way,
We must always remember to play after every storm.
All children are truly blessed
With the innocent gifts of gentleness,
Trust, and compassion,
To guide the wisdom of the grown-ups.
We all have a song in our heart
That inspires us in good times and hard times
If we take the time to listen.
   It matters, it matters,
   Oh, it matters that the world knows . . .
Our senses help discover the hidden and non-hidden
Enchantment of life if we use them.
We must carefully choose our words and wants
Or we could forever hurt others
With these dangerous weapons.
Strength and value of all things created
Must be measured by character and commitment
Rather than by might and by wealth.
   It matters, it matters,
   Oh, it matters that the world knows . . .
We must heed the lessons of everyday life
Through the celebration of
Children and Heartsongs, senses and words,
Or we could lose in our journey to the future.
   Oh, it matters . . .
   A person, by my name and being, existed
   With a strong spirit and an eternal mindset
   To become a peacemaker for all . . .
   By sharing the things that really matter.

By Mattie J.T. Stepanek, June 22, 2001, performed by Billy Gilman from *Music Through Heartsongs; Songs Based on the Poetry of Mattie J.T. Stepanek* (Sony Records, 2003)

On Growing Up (Part V)

We are growing up.
We are many colors of skin.
We are many languages.
We are many ages and sizes.
We are many countries . . .
But we are one earth.
We each have one heart.
We each have one life.
We are growing up, together,
So we must live as one family.

By Mattie J.T. Stepanek, September 22, 1996,
in *Journey Through Heartsongs*, (Hyperion/VSP, 2002)

Mattie enjoying time with his friends Andrew and Phillip Fall, spring 1995.

Mattie and his Hapkido instructor, Grandmaster Yong Sung Lee, with his championship trophy for the Black Belt division during the Battle of the USA, October 1999. In studying this Korean martial art, Mattie learned about Eastern culture, respect for self and others, and self-defense rather than offense as a means of protecting family and future.

Mattie learning about Native American culture from Art Shegonee and his daughter, Maral, during MDA Summer Camp, June 2002. The Shegonees are members of the Menominee/Potowatomi Tribe and peace activists.

Mattie was honored to serve as best man for his "kin-brother" Chris Dobbins in December 2002. During Chris and Cynthia Dobbins's wedding ceremony, Mattie also read the poem "Choice Vows," which was published in his *Loving Through Heartsongs* book.

THE MATTIE FLAG
SCHOOL ASSIGNMENT, OCTOBER 1998

At the center of the flag I designed to represent my life is a "Heartsong" because that is the symbol that guides my life. All of my poetry books have the word "Heartsongs" in the title. I believe if we all could listen to the song in our hearts, we can be peaceful, and so can the world. The heart is colored bright red to symbolize courage in the many personal battles of my life, like with disability, with death, and with divorce.

Behind the Heartsong is a sunset over the earth. My favorite color is "sunset," and the rays are colored orange and pink, which is the best part of the sunset. There are eight rays, because I am eight years old, an age I was never supposed to live long enough to see. Eight is made up of my favorite number, five, and my mother's favorite number, three. My mom and I are a family, and the numbers joined together make the special number eight. My name is in the rays of the sunset, because I am excited about living life.

The earth is colored in blues and grays of the sky and greens and browns of the ground. They are my mother's favorite colors. My mother and I are very close so I put our favorite colors right next to each other on my flag. The earth supports the sunset, and the sunset gives light to the earth. That's how my mom and I are with each other.

There are symbols on my flag, too. In the rays of the sunset are a rainbow and a pot of gold. The rainbow symbolizes happiness, and the pot of gold symbolizes the treasure we see when we look up to God instead of down into our pockets. I also like the color "treasure" and I enjoy the fantasy of digging for it at the beach.

In the bottom left corner are the "yin and yang" and "Hapkido" symbols. Yin and yang stands for harmony between people and things, and Hapkido stands for harmony throughout the world. Hapkido is a Korean martial art that means the way of combining the power of body, mind, and spirit for our world . . . for total peace and harmony. I have earned my First Degree Black Belt in Hapkido.

In the bottom right corner are the Star Wars Rebel Alliance Force symbol and the international peace symbol. The Star Wars sign symbolizes good and light forces winning over bad and dark forces. Star Wars books and movies are exciting fiction, but they represent the reality of conflict and the sad destruction of violence. The peace sign is important because when I grow up, I want to be a peacemaker. I want to be an ambassador for humanity, and travel all over the world teaching peace through my written and spoken words.

I really enjoyed this assignment, because it required me to think about things that really matter and about how I would want to be represented as I touch the world.

E-mail from: Bob Ross, President, Muscular Dystrophy Association
Date: October 6, 2003
To: Mattie Stepanek (cc: Jerry Lewis)
Re: Ambassadorship

Dear Mattie: I just heard the wonderful news! Thanks so much for agreeing to serve an unprecedented third term as MDA's 2004 National Goodwill Ambassador. There's no doubt that you're the right man for the job. Below are some excerpts from the press release we are issuing about your appointment. We're extremely grateful for the continued loyalty and enthusiastic support we've received from you and your mother. The both of you are very special people—we're glad we're family!

Love from all here, Bob

Teen Poet to Serve Rare Third Term as MDA Ambassador
Tucson, Arizona, October 6, 2003—One of the world's most remarkable teenagers, Mattie J.T. Stepanek, has agreed to serve a rare third term as National Goodwill Ambassador for the Muscular Dystrophy Association. Mattie, who lives in a Maryland suburb of Washington, D.C., with his mother, Jeni, is a best-selling poet who's also widely known for his passionate efforts at promoting peace and toler-ance. Although MDA's national ambassadors usually hold office for just one or two years, MDA officials were so delighted with Mattie's service to MDA for the past two years that they asked him to retain the title in 2004. He'll become only the sec-ond youngster to serve three terms and the first to do so in almost forty years.
  "Oh my gosh! This is amazing! This is awesome! I'm really surprised and hon-ored," was Mattie's enthusiastic response. Mattie, thirteen, and Jeni both have a rare disease related to muscular dystrophy called dysautonomic mitochondrial myopathy. The disease took the lives of Mattie's three siblings.
  "The words 'amazing' and 'outstanding' aren't enough to describe Mattie and the tremendous pride I feel to be his teammate in MDA's fight," MDA National Chairman Jerry Lewis said. "We're deeply grateful that this wise and gifted young man has agreed to continue his terrific and very effective work for MDA." Mattie is eager to continue spreading the word about MDA's mission, and to again represent MDA at special events and fund-raisers, as his health permits. "I love doing stuff for MDA and am glad that I can continue to help," Mattie said. His planned activities in 2003 were reduced by a four-month-long hospital stay in the spring due to respira-tory and other health complications caused by his disease. His overall health remains fragile, and he requires weekly platelet transfusions on an outpatient basis. Despite that setback, he took part in many local and national MDA events, including appear-ing via satellite from Baltimore on the 2003 Jerry Lewis MDA Telethon.

A poet since age three, Mattie is the best-selling author of numerous books of poetry. In 2003, he collaborated with another outstanding teen, fifteen-year-old singer Billy Gilman, on the CD *Music Through Heartsongs*. Gilman is MDA's National Youth Chairman. In addition to MDA events, Mattie's upcoming schedule includes book signings at Maryland bookstores in November, and one at the Kennedy Center in Washington in December. He'll also be a featured speaker at several special events on the East Coast, and is collaborating with President Jimmy Carter on a book about peacemaking.

Mattie's neuromuscular disease disrupts his body's autonomic functions, such as breathing, oxygen use, and digestion. He uses a power wheelchair and ventilator. Jeni Stepanek, who also uses a power wheelchair, has a milder, adult-onset form of the disease, and wasn't aware she was affected until all four of her children were born.

MDA is a voluntary health agency working to defeat more than forty neuro-muscular diseases through programs of worldwide research, comprehensive services, and far-reaching professional and public health education. The Association's programs are funded almost entirely by individual private contributors.

Mattie talks with Jerry Lewis in Las Vegas about the upcoming 2002 MDA Labor Day Telethon in Hollywood.

Mattie dances with camp director Katie McGuire at "Dance Night" during MDA Summer Camp, 2002.

Mattie enjoying time on the pier at Camp Maria with "Scuba Scott" and his counselor, Devin Dressman, 2002.

Mattie saying goodbye to his good friend Neil Dafner at the end of MDA Summer Camp week, 2003.

Mattie (the "whoopie cushion") poses with other teens and counselors from the MDA Baltimore Teen Group during a Halloween party, 2003. Mattie was a member of the advisory board for the group, which met monthly so that teens with neuromuscular disease had the opportunity to socialize or hear speakers invited to discuss relevant issues.

Jerry Lewis, Mattie, and Larry King share thoughts about the role of advocates and ambassadors for the MDA during the 2002 Labor Day Telethon.

Mattie and Jerry Lewis talk about the importance of the MDA and bringing hope to families during the 2002 National MDA Labor Day Telethon.

Mattie and Jerry Lewis celebrate another successful MDA Labor Day Telethon at the close of the show in 2002.

Mattie gets up close to the Jerry Lewis star on Hollywood Boulevard, August 2002.

Ed McMahon signs Mattie's "Signature Book" before the 2002 MDA Labor Day Telethon in Hollywood, California.

Mattie and Bruce Cunningham proudly show off their "matching co-host tuxes" during the Baltimore, Maryland, broadcast of the 2003 MDA Labor Day Telethon.

Mattie with friend and music artist Christopher Cross, who performed some of his hits at the 2004 Heartsongs Gala, and performed "Eternal Echoes," written by Mattie, during the 2005 Heartsong Gala.

Mattie with Ron Hemelgarn, President of Indy Racing League Hemelgarn Racing Team and recipient of a 2004 Heartsongs Gala Award.

Mattie with Billy Gilman at the 2003 Heartsongs Gala. Billy has performed songs at the gala from his CD *Music Through Heartsongs: Songs Based on the Poems of Mattie J.T. Stepanek* every year since the gala began.

Mattie with his best friend, Hope Wyatt, at the 2004 Heartsongs Gala. Since Mattie's death, Hope has made thousands of "Sunset Memorial Ribbons of Hope" to raise money for the MDA Mattie Fund.

Madison Cross helps Kaylee Dobbins paint her 2005 Heartsongs Gala keepsake T-shirt. In 2005, Madison recorded the song "He Was Just Like Me," written by her father, Christopher Cross, as a tribute to Mattie. One hundred percent of the iTunes and CD profits go to the MDA Mattie Fund.

Jan Cross, Jeni, Sandy Newcomb, and Madison Cross model their finished T-shirt designs.

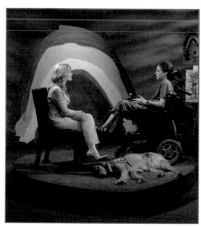

Mattie's mom, Jeni, and *Entertainment Tonight*'s Jann Carl talk about the MDA Mattie Fund during the filming of *Play After the Storm: Remembering Mattie Stepanek*. Mattie worked with Jann on many MDA projects, including the Jerry Lewis National Labor Day Telethon. The MDA Mattie Fund, which supports research in childhood neuromuscular diseases, was originally created in response to the sadness of Mattie's death, but has grown into a living fund for hope. This fund-raising endeavor has been so successful that two postdoctoral fellowships have been established in Mattie's name to support research directly in mitochondrial myopathies, which is the category of neuromuscular disease that led to the death of Mattie and his siblings.

Heaven's Smile

On New Year's Eve, look out at the moon
That will bring new tomorrows.
And if the moon is God's thumb-nail,
Then you can see Heaven's smile.
Know that the smile is a gift,
In the middle of the Angel-Stars
Watching over us from above.
Know that the cold air of winter brings us hugs,
As we keep tightly with each other for warmth.
If you understand this,
It will help you get wiser and stronger.
It will help our Heartsongs to grow.
It will help peace to spread in the world.
It will help Mother Earth to live another year.
And if you see a shooting star,
Know that it is very special
Even if we don't really get to wish on it.
Understand that the gift is to our heart, and
We can always wish within our heart.
My wish, even if it is only in my heart,
Is for a safer next year that is not so rough,
And that I am wishing on the eve of
A peaceful new year, and years.
So remember,
Every New Year's Eve, look up into the sky, and
See Heaven's smile in whatever moon is there.
It will be a reflection of life and love,
And a gift for you to meditate
About the past, the present, and our future,
As we get stronger in understanding each year.

By Mattie J.T. Stepanek, December 31, 1997,
in *Loving Through Heartsongs* (Hyperion/VSP, 2003)

E-mail from: Mattie J.T. Stepanek
Date: January 04, 2002 10:10 PM EST
To: Jimmy Carter
Subject: (no subject)

Hi Jimmy,

I hope you enjoyed your New Year! Congratulations! Your book is on the *New York Times* best-seller list!!! You are number NINE! That is great! You are also on other best-seller lists. And we are on a lot of lists together! You are nonfiction and I am fiction (even though my poetry is true or true wishes). I think one day, you and I should write a book together. "Poems and Passages for Peacemakers'" Or just "Peace." And it will be a collection of poems and essays and thoughts and quotes and whatever from both of us. Maybe world leaders and little children would want to read it, and learn a little bit more about peace and why it is one of the most important words in the world and for the world. One of these years, maybe we can do that.

My mom and I are listening to your book, *Christmas in Plains,* on tape. I love listening to you do the reading. It's really neat because we listened to it on the way to and from the studio where I recorded my books on tape! At first I wondered why I was recording my books. Then, while I was listening to you read your words, I realized why I should read my poetry for others to hear in my voice.

Well, I wonder if you stayed up to see the New Year in. I laughed about your experience when you were little, and were woken just at midnight, disappointed that nothing seemed different. I guess in some ways, you are right. And for children, I don't think that New Year's Eve needs to be any different than the eve of any other day of the year. But for many adults, I think New Year's Eve is very important. It's not just a good reason to get together with family or friends and have fun together. It's more important than that. I think that some people need a starting point, or a reason, or even an excuse, to resolve or resolute or embrace change. I believe that New Year's Eve gives people a moment to hope. To plan. To celebrate and anticipate something bigger and better than the year before. And to look back and remember and grow. That's why I like to stay up until midnight. The second it hits midnight is like any other second in time, except for what it symbolizes. We are so clearly right between the past and the future, and so aware of the present, which we all know is a gift. So I laughed when you spoke of your disappointment, because it is so true! Children are more aware of the present than adults ever are, and children believe in every moment. They are forgiving and accepting, and always ready to give a new chance or take one. So, for a child, especially one with a good life in spite of hardships, like you as a child, New Year's Eve should be a disappointment. But for me, making it to that midnight marker is a great thing!

Did you get any snow where you are? We got about an inch, but that was it. Ten miles south got a lot, and ten miles north got nothing. We were on the edge of it. It was pretty, though. We live in the basement of a house and our door looks out into the woods. It is so beautiful in every season, and when it snows, it looks like a fairy-tale scene from a book. I like where we live. There are no windows but it is bright. I have my own room and I feel very safe. I didn't feel safe before in our old basement apartment, which had a few small windows high up on the wall. I loved the people who owned the house, but I was afraid living there. I like having no windows now so we can't keep getting broken into like before. I like thinking about your childhood. I think everyone should read your new book, and think about the lessons. You said a lot of really important things, without it sounding like you were telling people what to think. That's a good way to teach people.

I love you. Please tell Mrs. Carter that I say hello, and Amy, and your family.

Love, Mattie

E-mail from: Jimmy Carter
Date: January 08, 2002 7:17 AM EST
To: Mattie J.T. Stepanek
Subject: Holiday, etc.

To Mattie: I'm glad you had a good holiday. As I mentioned in my book, our entire family (twenty-two of us) spent a week together, this time at Disney World, on a cruise ship, and on a private tour of the space shuttle program at Cape Canaveral. We drove down to Florida and back, and enjoyed the trip. The highlight of the entire vacation was Amy's two-year-old, Hugo, who had a wonderful time with Mickey Mouse, Buzz Lightyear, and other Disney characters. All of us (except Hugo) stayed up to celebrate the end of 2001, along with 2,700 other passengers on the ship.

Plains had two inches of snow while we were at Canaveral, but most of it had melted before we arrived back home. This much snow only comes about every ten years.

I'm glad you decided to read your book. It adds a lot to have the author/poet do this, and I've read eight or ten of mine. *An Hour Before Daylight* is the third one nominated for a Grammy Award. If you need any of mine, let me know.

I have some days at home now, and am helping to supervise the renovation of three buildings on our main street that will be an antique mall and a small inn. It's a big job, but will mean a lot to our town when it's in operation. Also, I'm making a four-poster bed for the Carter Center to auction when we have our ski weekend in Colorado next month. This is a difficult job, especially forming the octagonal posts. As you know, I make something in my wood shop each year to raise money for the Center. I also stay involved in what's going on with our programs, and work on my novel to fill in the time gaps.

I'm always glad to hear from you. I love you, and am very proud of the beautiful and peaceful impact you have had on the people of our nation.

With love, and best wishes, Jimmy

Mattie receiving the 2002 Children's Hope Medal of Honor at the Washington, D.C., Children's National Medical Center, with Senator Barbara Ann Mikulski (D-MD) and Ellis Goodman (founder of the award).

Mattie doing a peace poetry reading for First Lady Laura Bush at the U.S. Capitol during the 2002 Annual Luncheon for Senate Spouses.

Pinch of Peace

Dear God,
Tonight my prayers are for the world.
We have to stop this fighting.
We have to stop the wars.
People need to lay down their weapons,
And find peace in their hearts.
People need to stop arguing and hating.
People need to notice the good things.
People need to remember You, God.
Maybe You could come and
Shoot a little bow-and-arrow pinch
Into all the angry people's hearts, God.
Then they would feel You again.
And then they would realize what
They are doing and how horrible the
Killing and hating and fighting is,
And they might even begin to pray.
Then, they could reach in, and
Pull the little bow-and-arrow pinch
Out of their hearts and feel good
And be loving and living people again.
And then,
The world would be at peace, and
The children would be safe, and
The people would be happy, and
We could all say "thank You" together.
Amen.

By Mattie J.T. Stepanek, March 25, 1996,
in *Heartsongs* (Hyperion/VSP, 2001)

The Mosaic Shattered

Hope is a present
Of future each day,
A voice from our heart
To show us the way.

Excerpt from "About Hope," May 21, 2003,
by Mattie J.T. Stepanek, in *Reflections of a Peacemaker:
A Portrait Through Heartsongs*
(Andrews McMeel Publishing, 2005)

Vietnam War Memorial

A wall gives structure.
It can divide and block.
It can support and fortify.
It can be a place to display
Photos, writings, awards,
And memories.
But this, is The Wall.
The Wall that gives structure
To the insane losses of a war.
The Wall that represents
A nation divided and blocked.
The Wall that supports too
Many broken hearts and bodies.
The Wall that fortifies the reality
Of dead lives among the living.
The Wall that reflects memories
Of what was, of what is,
Of what might have been,

In photos, in letters and poems,
In medals of honor and dedication,
And in teddy bears, and flowers,
And tears and tears and tears.
This is The Wall,
Born out of pain and anguish
And guilt,
That gives names to the children
Of grieving mothers and fathers
And to the spouses of widows
And to parents of wondering children.
This is The Wall
That echoes sadness and fear,
Yet whispers relief and hope.
This is The Wall.
May we be forever blessed by its
Structure and fortitude and support,
And may we be forever reminded
Of the eternal divisions of war.

By Mattie J.T. Stepanek, February 4, 2000,
in *Journey Through Heartsongs*
(Hyperion/VSP, 2002)

E-mail from: Mattie J.T. Stepanek
Date: January 18, 2002 10:30 PM EST
To: Jimmy Carter
Subject: (no subject)

Dear Jimmy,

I just wanted to tell you that I was thinking about you and that I still love you. Sometimes, even though I have read so much about you and now have talked with you so many times, I just stop and think and my spirit feels so full, even when things seem so hard. You make me really think about things that matter in life. And I think about them in different ways.

You know that I want to be a peacemaker and I am doing my best to help people just stop for a minute and think. Think and be for themselves and for others and for the world. And I know that I should be peaceful with everyone, but it's also not smart to put yourself in a dangerous situation. Like even though I would want to talk to Osama Bin Laden about peace and the future, I wouldn't want to be alone with him in his cave . . . [I've had a personal experience of someone who has scared me and even hurt me.] I can't do something unsafe . . . My mom says that it is wrong for me to think bad things about [others], but she understands why it is not wrong for me to not want to see . . . or be with [someone who has hurt or scared me]. So I hope that you are still proud of me some, and that you don't think I am not being nice or a peacemaker.

We are supposed to have snow tomorrow in Maryland. Are you still in Georgia? My mom said that we can go there sometime, and see Plains. Is Archery near Plains? Do you still visit with your friends who you played with when you were very young? I laughed really hard when I read in your book about Amy and her friend thinking they had privacy from the secret service guys! How is the furniture coming along that you are building?

A lot of people I know have started reading books by or about you because I tell them what a good person you are. That makes me proud. Please tell Rosalynn that I said hello to her, and Amy and Hugo, too.

Love, Mattie

E-mail from: Jimmy Carter
Date: January 19, 2002 3:09 PM EST
To: Mattie J.T. Stepanek
Subject: (no subject)

Mattie: I'm delighted to hear from you, and you will notice that I'm responding directly to you. We only give our e-mail address to members of our family, but I want you to have it also . . . Just today, I've finished building the four-poster bed to be auctioned off for the Carter Center next month during our annual ski weekend. This is an ambitious project, and took more than 100 hours of work in my shop. I really enjoy designing and building things, but don't like the sanding and finishing. I've also made a photo album to go with the bed, with about three dozen pictures that I took of myself during construction.

We're also continuing work to revitalize the downtown area of Plains, and I look forward to showing it to you and your mother.

Mattie, you need not feel guilty about your feelings toward [someone who has hurt or scared you], if [someone] has done something in the past to make you [or your mother or someone you love] afraid . . .

To answer your other questions, Archery is just two and a half miles west of Plains, but nothing much is left there except my boyhood farm, St. Mark's AME Church, and a historical marker honoring Bishop William Johnson. I still see some of the folks who grew up with me out there, and we enjoy talking about old times. In fact, some of the things in my books have come out of these reminiscences.

Love, and best wishes, Jimmy

E-mail from: Mattie J.T. Stepanek
Date: January 21, 2002 6:18 AM EST
To: Jimmy Carter
Subject: (no subject)

Dear Jimmy,

I promise that I will not share your e-mail address with anyone. I've never shared the other one with anybody either. My mom told me that an e-mail address must always be given out by the person who owns it and not by friends, but I would have known that for somebody like you anyway.

[Your offer to listen to me and support me is very helpful. Some very frightening things have happened in my personal life.] . . . you really can't imagine some of the things that [have] happened [to me] and I know other kids have had it worse, but for me, [it is very scary] . . . thank you for offering [your support]. I will not dwell on [negative people and events from my past] anymore with you because I know being peaceful is better, and I don't want you to think that I am not a good person who gives others a chance. So I will not bring it up anymore, but please please trust me that I am not just being a mean kid . . .

It sounds like you are very good at building things. I like it that you and your wife made furniture when you were first married. Sometimes I think everyone should struggle just a little bit with money so that they appreciate just a teeny bit of the stresses too many people live with. My mom and I have had hard times . . . especially before we had a good support system set up. We didn't make our furniture, but we lived in someone's basement and mostly used what was there. Now we live in a different basement that seems bigger, and there's no mice and not as many spiders. Other than mice and spiders (and some kids teasing me at school), the hardest thing about being poor was the first few times we had to get food boxes from church. I learned that some people who donate food anonymously to an organization just give what is expired or what they wouldn't like to eat from their cabinets. Like we had lots of cans of garbanzo beans and black olives and boxes of food with dates on them from a while before we received them. But if you get "adopted" by another family in our church then the food is really good food. For the last three Christmases, we have been adopted by Mrs. Moi (we don't know her, just her name). She gave us the best of everything—great food, and wrapped gifts for me AND my mom! It was like she was shopping for herself and her own child. If we can get things cleared up with my book money and use a little bit of it, next Christmas my mom and I are going to be the ones to adopt a family. We will give the best food and gifts. We will give what we would want for our own family. My mom and I do OK now and we have good support, but I think it's good that I understand a bit of what many people go through in an even worse way. I think that's why you are such a good person, too. You worked hard for things and did things in a fair way, and you remember all that in what you still do now. I am very proud of you.

I had to have lab tests done last week because my dysautonomia was a little worse and I am needing more oxygen than before. I am right on the line for needing another blood transfusion. I am brave with a lot of things, but that's the one other thing that I am afraid of . . . I can be very brave with bruises and even knowing that I am probably going to live a whole lot less years than I want. But needles and sharp things just are horrible. But for the first time, I did OK. I cried, but I cooperated. I held out my arm and counted and did what I needed to do. I didn't feel good knowing that I have to do it again, but I feel good knowing that I did the best I've ever done in my life with it.

I hope that your family is all doing well. We got a few inches of snow here yesterday. It was so beautiful. Even today while it's melting it looks magical. Have a good week. I love you.

Love, Mattie

E-mail from: Mattie J.T. Stepanek
Date: February 02, 2002 2:51 PM EST
To: Jimmy Carter
Subject: (no subject)

Dear Jimmy,

How have you been doing? I was in the hospital again this week for blood transfusions. It hurt and I was scared, but I was the bravest I have ever been. It was also the first time in a long time that I actually came back home from the hospital without going into a crisis and almost dying! I wasn't doing well, I was needing more oxygen (I am on 70 percent so that's higher than you can safely go) so they decided to give me more blood to help carry the oxygen. They still don't know if it is going to help, but they know that I came back home!

I wrote a real neat essay for school this week. I didn't want to do it at first, but my mom said it was an assignment and I had no choice. It was hard because I didn't want to feel the feelings I would feel to write it. I had to write a first person essay about being the descendant of a slave. I had to explore positive and negative feelings, and talk about the dark past, and the hope of the future. It was sad to even think about it, but my mom said that's sometimes how we learn. I did learn. I learned to understand what someone else's Heartsong sounded like, and how it kept them going so many sad and unfair years ago.

Please tell your family I said hello. I will write to you again. I love you.

Love, Mattie

E-mail from: Jimmy Carter
Date: February 04, 2002 6:00 AM EST
To: Mattie J.T. Stepanek
Subject: (no subject)

To Mattie: I'm glad you came through the fearsome hospital visit so well, and am praying that the transfusion will have the desired effect.

Many of the black friends of my boyhood are still my neighbors, so I am reminded often of the times when U.S. citizens, our Supreme Court, the Congress, and almost all American churches approved and supported the official segregation practices of our country. They are all descendants of slaves, and now have good lives in the Plains community, but many of their families still have to bear the burden of those 100 years of racial discrimination. Maybe you could send me a copy of your essay.

We'll be spending the last part of this week on our annual ski event in Colorado.

You can read about it on our Web site (www.cartercenter.org). Rosalynn and I still ski, but quite carefully now at our age. This is a lot of fun, with about 300 of our friends and a group of Future Force kids, but primarily designed to raise money to support our Center's projects. Our annual budget is about $30 million, so this is a constant responsibility for me.

I'm still spending a lot of my time while in Plains working on the project to build a small (seven-room) inn and an antique mall. This will help to revitalize the downtown area of the town. We'll be saving one of the suites for you and Jeni whenever you all can come to see us.

All our family are doing well, and very proud of my personal friendship with you.

Write me when you can, and remember that I love you, think of you often, and am praying for your better health.

Jimmy

PS I'm sending you my taped copies of *Living Faith* and *Sources of Strength,* which you may enjoy in your spare time.

Mattie displaying the "What Would Mommy Do?" card he made for his mom, Mother's Day, 2002.

Mattie with U.S. Department of Health and Human Services Secretary Tommy Thompson during a Harley-Davidson Motorcycle fund-raising event for MDA in Milwaukee, Wisconsin, July 2002.

Congressman Jim Moran (D-VA) congratu-lates Mattie on receiving the "Points of Light" Humanitarian Award from Children's Hospice International, recognizing Mattie's years of lobbying on Capitol Hill for the implementation of the "PACC Model" (Program of All-Inclusive Care for Children and Families), September 2003.

Mattie receiving the Humanitarian Award from Claude Allen, assis-tant secretary of the Department of Health and Human Services, on Capitol Hill during Disability Awareness Month, October 2003.

Post-Terrorism Haiku

Let us remember . . .
We are the land of the free,
Not of the vengeful.

Let us remember . . .
That it is in God we trust,
Not in bombs and guns.

Let us remember . . .
Peace grows from a gentle heart,
Not one filled with spite.

By Mattie J.T. Stepanek, September 12, 2001,
in *Celebrate Through Heartsongs*
(Hyperion/VSP, 2002)

Mattie celebrating freedom and fellowship.

E-mail from: Mattie J.T. Stepanek
Date: June 18, 2002 8:39 PM EST
To: Jimmy Carter
Subject: (no subject)

Hello, this is Mattie's mom. I apologize for the delay in this note. Mattie wrote it to you a week ago on his little computer and asked me to transfer it to a computer with e-mail and send it. I forgot until tonight. He is at the MDA Summer Camp this week. But I will let him know it was sent to you tonight. Thank you, and take care, Jeni Stepanek

Dear Jimmy,

How have you been? You've been very busy. Did you know that at the same time that you were talking peace in Cuba, I was giving a keynote address to 5,200 children and adults about peace at the Children's Peace Pavilion in Missouri? You and I were in the paper together about peace because of that! My theme was "Peace Is Possible" and I had three easy steps to peace. And you were trying to promote peace in Cuba at the same time. We were doing the same thing! I am sorry that President Bush didn't back you in the way he could have. I respect him as a president, but I don't always agree with how he is handling things. I wouldn't want you to be president again because I love you and I think it's too dangerous. But I want our current president to listen to you as a peacemaker. I don't think it's safe for anyone to be president right now. So I guess he's brave for doing the job. But he . . . says two different things at once. It's confusing to me. I hope your family is doing well and that your grandchildren aren't playing too many practical jokes on the parents (some are good, though!). I love you very much and I am so proud of your work.

Love, Mattie

E-mail from: Jimmy Carter
Date: June 19, 2002 7:47 AM EST
To: Mattie J.T. Stepanek
Subject: (no subject)

Mattie: It is good to hear from you, and a pleasure and honor for me to know that you and I are involved in peacemaking at the same time. We have been to South Africa after returning from Cuba, on our annual "Jimmy Carter Work Project" to build Habitat for Humanity homes for poor families. Rosalynn and I had 4,300 other volunteers join us, and we completed 100 homes in the five days we were in

Durban. After that, we went northward in KwaZulu Natal province to rest, look for birds, learn about the history of the Zulu people, and look at some wild animals. This morning, we're on the way to Atlanta, where I continue to run the Carter Center and am now finishing my twentieth year as a professor at Emory University.

I think of you often, especially because people are constantly expressing their admiration for "Your young friend, Mattie." Needless to say, this friendship really means a lot to me. I hope you're doing well, taking care of yourself, and enjoying both your extensive campaign for peace and also the quiet times with your mom. All of our family are doing well (four children and eleven grandchildren), and we stay in close touch with them either with direct visits or by e-mail.

I don't think you need to worry about danger to the president. I know from experience that he is one of the best protected people in the world. I never felt uncomfortable or fearful when I was in the White House. As do other private citizens, I always respect the presidents, appreciate their service, but reserve the right to express my own views in as positive a manner as possible.

Write when you can. I'm always interested in what you are doing.

Love, Jimmy

E-mail from: Mattie J.T. Stepanek
Sent: December 14, 2002
To: Jimmy Carter
Subject: (no subject)

Dear Jimmy,

Thank you so much for picking me up such a perfect rock. [After giving his acceptance speech in Oslo, Norway, for the Nobel Peace Prize, Jimmy Carter was thinking of Mattie and went outside and picked up a rock for him (see page 169).] It will be the best one in my collection. (It replaces what will now be the second-best one, which is a piece of the crumbling Berlin Wall.) I can't wait to talk with you again when you and your family are finished vacationing and traveling. I am just so proud for you, and it makes me so excited about what we can do with other people in the world.

Love, Mattie

Unfinished

Seeping silently in the night
Dark before the sun's first light
The deuce of death not yet in sight
Life awaiting dawn . . .
Fires, fires, fires fell
The horror, a sight straight from hell
Why fire attacks, it will never tell
Death before the dawn . . .
Life cries out for help from friends
Will the hatred ever end?
The screams of frightened souls will send
Desperate prayer to survive 'til dawn . . .
The fires, the fires, slowly die down
Ending their horrendous sound
Secure-like feeling will soon come 'round
Arriving with the dawn . . .
From fire and fear
Such presence so near
To peace of a dove
Some future, some year
And yet we still ponder
The next day, what next . . .
Live in fear or choose fight
Live in fear or choose might
Live in fear or choose flight
Why choose any such sight
For not one is right
If we choose to count
On this and each night . . .
To wake with another dawn.

By Mattie J.T. Stepanek, March 24, 2003,
in *Reflections of a Peacemaker: A Portrait Through Heartsongs*
(Andrews McMeel Publishing, 2005)

THE RAGES AND WAGES OF WAR

War. It is a strong word. It is a deep, complex, and provoking word. It is a word that makes some people cheer, some people cry, and some people pause to consider the future. Conflict between "right and wrong" or even "good and evil" has existed since the beginning of humanity, and free will. And too often, these struggles lead to violence and war. And violence and war too often lead to death, destruction, darkness, anger, and other unnecessary falls of life.

Even though it has always been pursued, I do not believe that there has ever been a time in recorded history when there was true world peace, or even true peace among all groups of people within a nation. Because of the ongoing reality of war, and because of the great desire of so many people to seek peace for individuals and for the world, many questions weigh heavily on my mind. Why does conflict exist, and why does it so often lead to violence and war? What are common causes of war? Are the sources of conflict and war different today than in past decades and centuries? How is the act of war different today than in previous eras? Is the violence of war ever really necessary? Can war ever be justified? Why does the United States choose to support intervention, even declare war, in some situations, but not others? And, how can we create the possibility, and the reality, of peaceful conflict resolutions within and between individuals, families, communities, and countries? Answering questions of war, and seeking solutions, resolutions leading to peace, must begin with an examination of issues.

The rages and wages of war are like all other important matters, requiring both contemplation and comprehension. To achieve peace, we must consider the causes and consequences of a lack of peace. I have studied books and articles describing the grounds, the battles, the outcomes, and the devastating and deadly expenses of many different wars. I have ruminated on written and spoken words, deliberations, and lessons of war victims, and of war survivors. I have reviewed documentaries and movies that analyze aspects and remind generations of the causes and costs of war.

I do not have the absolute answers to questions of war. But, I have formed thoughts and opinions, based on information and reasoning. I have studied conflict and violence and examined the justifications we use for war. And still, I do not understand how we end up in the devastating and unnecessary reality of war, again and again and again. And yet, we do.

CONFLICT AND VIOLENCE

Conflict is not the same as violence. Conflict involves tension, and comes from some type of disagreement, discord, or dispute. Conflict is a difference of judgment on issues between two or more people, or groups of people. And, conflict is normal. We all have thoughts, and opinions, and preferences, which at times will differ from those of others. Part of growing up is learning to deal with conflicts that arise inside of ourselves, or with other people. Conflict does not need to be considered negative, or necessarily leading to arguments, fights, violence, or retaliation. There are many ways to resolve conflict, and conflict resolution can often lead to changes and improvements that benefit individuals, or communities, or countries.

Violence involves hostility, threats, aggression, brutality, and fighting of some sort. Some violence hurts people's bodies, some violence hurts people's minds, and some violence hurts people's spirits. Violence can also destroy people's belongings, their land, their culture, and even their futures. Unlike conflict, which is an inevitable disagreement in thought or reason on occasion, violence does not need to be considered a normal or natural or necessary consequence of conflict. War, therefore, which involves some type of violence, is not necessary for conflict resolution.

Although conflict and violence mean different things, they are rooted in and grow from similar sources. Differences in attitudes and habits, and in thoughts and opinions, can often be the source of disagreements. The veracity of emotions like pride, prejudice, fear, jealousy, and egocentrism, are also common starting places for discord. Many people are not satisfied with who they are as a person or with what they own as possessions. Many people compare themselves to others, or to the standards of others. This lack of satisfaction or lack of security—physical, emotional, economic, spiritual—can then lead to conflict within or between individuals.

Violence, and war, grow from these same types of personal, or societal, or worldly conflicts, with the analyzed roots often sorted into categories such as economics, territorial battles, power struggles, cultural or religious clashes, and human or civil rights. Thus, the sources of conflict, and of violence and war, are similar in that they begin with some basic need or desire or comparison of one person or group to another. When an individual or a group does not have some basic need met, or does feel that basic needs are being met appropriately, the conflict may grow, even fester, and without support and attention, the conflict may result in violence and war.

The sources of conflict, and of violence and war, are really no different today than in past decades and centuries. We fight for land and we fight for power. We fight over natural resources and we fight over human rights. We fight in the name of pride, and we even fight in the name of religion. But so often, the land we are fighting over is ravaged, the natural resources are wasted, and the humans we seek to defend are destroyed. All religions support peace, yet we use them as grounds for conflict and violence. And fighting over religion has never made any sense to me at all. How can we fight over something that is based in unprovable faith, and that serves the purpose of inspiring us through life to our hopefully glorious, but unknown, eternal future?

THE ACT AND JUSTIFICATION OF WAR

Although the causes of war have not changed across time, the rules and weapons of war have changed greatly. Centuries ago, war was considered necessary and honorable by many. And while serving to protect human and civil rights is still a necessary and honorable profession, the act of war is so different today that the rages and wages of why and how we fight, and alternatives to violent response to conflict, must be reconsidered.

In wars of past eras, men would march to a battlefield with a musket or a sword, knowing that they were going to that planned place of battle to live or to die for a cause in hand-to-hand and face-to-face combat. But we have made so many advancements in science and technology across the years. And sadly, while we have used discoveries and inventions for the improvement of humanity and living, we also used these same discoveries and inventions to evolve the devastating act and escalating destructiveness of war.

War is different now than it was in history, because it can be deadlier to victims, and it can be accomplished from an impersonal distance by those declaring victory. Though we did not develop ways to grow past our needs and desires that lead to war, the rules and weapons of war have greatly changed. There is no respectfully defined battlefield. There is no public announcement or warning about when and where a war will begin. And while we have created "smart" bombs that are aimed to target particular locations and buildings, even the smartest bomb cannot detect human life and avoid human casualty. Men, women, and even children are drawn into battles, sometimes without choice.

War today occurs in a surprised city of innocent people, in a restaurant or office building, on street corners and buses, even in schools and places of worship. And now, we do not march with a handful of small weapons to win or lose at personal gain or pain. Rather, we have bombs that can blow up and destroy a state or country in an instant, and spread fire and sickness even further into territory and time. We have capsules that release chemicals into the air to spread deadly diseases across a nation or continent, so that a whole population, an entire culture, will slowly or quickly, and unexpectedly or painfully, be wasted and killed. Indeed, the location of war has moved from battlefields to backyards, and the methods of war have evolved from arrows to anthrax, from swords to seron gas, and from muskets to weapons of mass destruction.

Considering the evolution of the rages of war makes it easy for me to say that we, as a world of people, cannot risk the wages of war any longer. But some will argue that war is still justified, or necessary, for a particular cause. A difficult question must be considered then: "Can we ever justify war?" Many people seeking peace, including myself, would initially respond with a quick "no." But, if that is the correct answer, how can I say that the ancestors of my country had a right to fight for independence in the American Revolution? How can I agree with the battles to keep my country together and to abolish slavery during the United States Civil War? And how can I defend the decisions of my country's leaders to unite with half the world and fight against tyranny and mass murder during World Wars I and II? And perhaps because I was born and raised as a free citizen in this country, I can see the justification for fighting for each of those causes.

The independence and civil rights of many countries, of many cultures, of many individuals, have occurred as a result of war or violence. We celebrate victories with national holidays and commemorations. We cheer at parades and reflect at monuments dedicated to remembering and honoring those who fought for our safety, our needs, our desires, our freedoms. How, then, can I reason, and believe, and advocate that war is not justifiable today, when the causes are the same for the people of other nations now as they were for people in my own nation years ago?

I do not disagree at all with people having their needs, and even some desires that don't interfere with the needs and desires and dignity of others, met in appropriate ways. I must admit that there are things worthy of conflict, especially meeting the basic needs and rights of all people. However, I do not believe that conflict must lead to violence, or to war. I also believe that even if war seemed justifiable in the past, due to the changes in how we battle, the risks of war are no longer justifiable, even though the age-old sources of conflict need to be addressed and resolved. We, as a world, must seek to meet and balance the basic needs and rights of all people, and to accept and resolve the reality of conflicts in nonviolent ways. We must seek peace, rather than resort to war.

SEEKING PEACE

One of my favorite quotes comes from the character Yoda in a *Star Wars* movie: "Fear leads to anger, anger leads to hate, and hate leads to suffering." This is so true. So very true. This saying is helpful to me because when I am scared or angry about something, or when my feelings are hurt by someone, I remember that "hate" is a strong word, and once said, it can never be taken back, even with an apology. We can move and grow beyond something that is said or done. We can even apologize or forgive. But once something is said or done, we cannot change history. The fact of pain and suffering can never be taken back. But, we can search for ways to feel less afraid, and to feel and be stronger, safer, more secure.

Our world is in a crisis. There is so much anger, so much hatred, so much fighting. People worry about differences, but our differences are our unique beauties, our strengths, our gifts. We compare ourselves to others, measuring might and wealth and success and esteem in units that don't really count or add up in the standards of future and eternity. I fear the rages, and the wages, of war. And sometimes, I think the world might need fictional characters— like Yoda from *Star Wars*, and Gandalf from *The Lord of the Rings*, and Professor Dumbledore from *Harry Potter*—who battle defensively, gently overcoming oppression and injustice, to come to life and inspire people to think and act and be differently. Then, rather than letting our fear lead to anger and then hate and then suffering, people would be more inclined to have courage and wisdom and seek peace in nonviolent methods like the heroes in books and movies. But in reality, we have people and organizations with all the admirable qualities of these fictional role models. People of all nations, of all ages, of all races and religions and abilities and aspirations can choose to just look around in our very real world, and see that we are a mosaic of unique gifts. But we must heed that the mosaic is breaking. The treasured pieces are scattered. We need to gather, and we need to rebuild the mosaic of life. We need to be motivated to choose peace.

Peace is possible. I have seen organizations and individuals around the world reach out and make a positive difference during natural disasters and during catastrophic events that result from human choice. But too often, these efforts are short-lived and our attentions are averted to some other situation. Humans are born good, and we generally want to live a good life. Attaining peace, for one's self and one's family and one's world is a common goal for most people. But like any other endeavor, it is time consuming and takes understanding, consideration, and effort. Planning and engaging in war is a complex and risky affair. Although planning and embracing peace would seem to be the simple absence of violence, creating and maintaining world peace while meeting the basic needs of all people is even more complex than war. However, waging peace, rather than war, is also more just.

Peace is equitable. Achieving peace, for individuals, for communities, for countries, requires meeting the basic needs and rights of all people in a fair, unbiased, and reasonable way. Achieving peace involves balancing needs, even desires, so that individual or group gains are not at the cost of the basic needs or rights of any other individual or group. Achieving peace is a simple yet noble concept, but one that compels us to think and to speak and to act gently, creatively, and unselfishly.

Peace is worthy, and peace is just. I am not alone in my thoughts, or in my efforts to strive for peace. There are many organizations and individuals from around the world who welcome the challenge of seeking peace for all people in all nations. Together we will gently remind the world—the leaders and the children—that peace is possible, because peace is a choice. Our attitudes are a choice. Our habits are a choice. How we touch the world is a choice. Peace is a way of thinking and being and living, and, therefore, peace is a choice. And there are many role models from many walks of life from whom we can learn as we choose to plan peace.

Mattie discussing issues of self-defense and world peace at the Pentagon with General Richard Myers, vice chairman of the Joint Chiefs of Staff, October 2000. Myers was later appointed chairman and maintained communication and friendship with Mattie.

Mattie giving a presentation on "Peer Mediation in the School System" with his elementary school counselor Mollie Thorn in Chicago, Illinois, May 2002. Mattie was later presented with the Social Interest Award from the North American Society of Adlerian Psychology during the conference.

9-11 . . . 2001

It was a dark day in America.
There was no amazing grace.
Freedom did not ring.
Tragedy attacked sky-high.
Fiery terror reigned.
Structures collapsed.
Red with blood, white with ash,
And out-of-the-sky blue.
As children trust elders,
Citizens find faith in leaders.
But all were blinded,
Shocked by the blasts.
Undefiable outrage.
Undeniable outpouring
Of support, even prayer,
Or at least, moments of silence.
Church and State
Could not be separated.
A horrific blasting of events
With too few happy endings.
Can the children sleep
Safely in their beds tonight?
Can the citizens ever rest
Assured of national security again?
God, please, bless America . . .
And the rest of our earthly home.

By Mattie J.T. Stepanek, September 11, 2001,
in *Hope Through Heartsongs*
(Hyperion/VSP, 2002)

E-mail from: Mattie J.T. Stepanek
Sent: September 18, 2001 9:05 AM EST
To: International Association of Fire Fighters and MDA
Subject: 9/11 tragedy and prayer

Dear Fire Fighters and other supporters of the Muscular Dystrophy Association:

One week ago today, a terrible tragedy happened in this country. We were attacked by terrorists. Thousands of lives were lost. Innocent people died. Children and adults. Military personnel and civilians. Cleaning crews and business leaders. Mommies and daddies and spouses and neighbors and friends and many more. And so very sadly, hundreds of fire fighters who rushed bravely to try and help save the innocent people who may still have a chance to survive.

Hundreds and hundreds of fire fighters went in again and again to do anything they could to help save as many lives as possible. They must have been afraid that the buildings could fall on them. Some of the largest airplanes had crashed into some of the tallest buildings and caused one of the hottest fires imaginable. But they were true heroes. Even in the smoke of the fires, we could see clearly why the USA is called the home of the brave—look at all the members of the New York Fire Department who put their duty and other people's lives first.

I am especially sad because just a day and a half before this horrible event, my mom and I spent a wonderful weekend with hundreds and hundreds of fire fighters who played softball for three days to raise money for the Muscular Dystrophy Association and "Jerry's Kids." One of the NYFD teams came in second place for the whole tournament. At the closing ceremonies, a player from that team handed me his trophy. I touch that trophy now, praying for all of the lost lives, remembering the generosity and bravery of the fire fighters, and wondering . . . is the player who handed me his trophy one of the hundreds of fire fighters who are still missing?

Now, we must go on. My philosophy in life has always been: "Remember to play after every storm." That's not always easy to do, but it is the only way life can survive. But, as life goes on, I have a prayer and a wish. My prayer and my wish are that these thousands of people and hundreds of fire fighters have not died without a lesson for our country. My prayer and my wish are that we place meaning in this great loss. My prayer and my wish are that we always remember how our country suddenly united after a tragedy, and how we all reached out to pray and help and be with our neighbors. As we go on and live and play, as we must, please let us all remember our response to this loss, and let us take that unity and fellowship with us into the future.

With love and respect and appreciation,
Mattie Joseph Thaddeus Stepanek
MDA National Goodwill Ambassador

Mattie with Jack Ginty at the Uniformed Fire Fighter Association headquarters next to Ground Zero in New York City, February 2002. Mattie presented Jack with a signed copy of his "9/11 poetry" and Jack presented Mattie with the fire fighter clothes he was wearing on September 11, 2001, when he crawled out of the collapsed World Trade Center buildings after the terrorist attacks.

Mattie enjoying time with fire fighter buddies Bert "Bubba" Mentrassi (Greenburgh, NY) and "JJ" Jackson (Mississauga, Canada) during the 2002 MDA/ IAFF Softball Tournament. In June 2004, they would lift Mattie's casket onto the back of a fire truck and accompany him on his "last ride."

Mattie talks with IAFF General President Harold Schaitberger, after giving an inspirational speech at the organization's 2002 Las Vegas convention.

E-mail from: Mattie J.T. Stepanek
Sent: September 11, 2002 10:04 AM EST
To: Jeni Stepanek
Subject: 9/11 Anniversary Composition

Trading Ideas: A Letter to Whom It May Concern

Every year, we must recognize the tragedies that occurred on September 11, 2001, in some way. We must commemorate the lives lost in the New York World Trade Center, in the Pentagon, and in the Pennsylvania field where airline passengers prevented another deadly attack on Washington, D.C. However, if we focus on the terrorism and evilness of the day, it not only means that Americans will never move on and heal their wounds, but it also means that in a way, we are giving undue credit to the attackers who caused pain to so many thousands of innocent people. Thus, instead of only mourning and merely reading countless speeches of sadness, we must rise out of the ashes and create a day that reminds us of how life could be and, in fact, should be.

What I am proposing is a true "World Trade Day" that will annually occur on September 11. People around the world will find some way to trade something significant, though not necessarily financially pricey, with someone else. One person might choose to trade a photograph of a loved one with a neighbor, another may choose to trade a game with someone at a bus stop, and yet another might choose to trade a book or a positive idea with someone in a distant country. This act of kindness and sharing can help Americans unite closer with each other, and spread a message of hope and peace around the planet. Imagine . . . a just peace could simply begin with trading thoughts over a cup of tea and a game of chess. How could we not seek such a tradition, in which we transform terror and tragedy into tranquility and trust?

The new "World Trade Day" can foster relations between and among people of all ages and nationalities and beliefs. Children can trade with adults. Israelis can trade with Palestinians. Catholics can trade with Muslims. Anyone can trade with any other person . . . and that is what is important about this event. In commemorating a tragic event in a way that promotes positive growth, we can move beyond our anger and fears without forgetting the truth of the past. By celebrating "World Trade Day" with a respectful and future-oriented attitude, we are paying the highest honor to those who suffered on September 11, 2001, and we are planting seeds of peace for all those who will live through the future of September 11 each year.

E-mail from: Mattie J.T. Stepanek
Sent: September 11, 2003 11:05 AM EST
To: Jeni Stepanek
Subject: 9/11 Anniversary Composition

Anniversary Reactions

    What is an anniversary? The dictionary defines it as "the date on which an event took place in a previous year or in the past." People enjoy celebrating or remembering anniversaries, for they can serve as a sign of coming of age, a lasting foundation, or just a festive recollection of an event worth remembering. Classic examples of such commemorations include a birthday party when we celebrate the joy of someone growing up and getting older, or a wedding anniversary party when we celebrate a married couple growing and remaining together for another year.

    An anniversary is not always remembering a happy occasion, though. We may also have reason to commemorate an unfortunate or sad event such as a death anniversary, when people come together to remember a loved one on the day he or she died. Another example of an unhappy anniversary can be that of a tragic event, like the start of a horrible war, or a major riot, or the loss of thousands of lives from a single cruel act.

    Today happens to be an anniversary. And it happens to be a sad and tragic one. This is the second anniversary of September 11, 2001. Why would people especially recognize and remember one random day? What made September 11, 2001, stand out from all of the other September elevenths that have happened year after year in the past?

    Two years ago on this day, thousands of innocent people lost their lives to vicious and deadly terrorist attacks on the United States. People from another part of the world hijacked four American airplanes, each with hundreds of men, women, and children on board, and kamikazied into different parts of America. One plane crashed into the Pentagon building in Washington, D.C. One crashed into an open field in Pennsylvania, because the brave innocents on board overpowered the terrorists, so that they could prevent another building from being attacked. And two planes crashed into the World Trade Center in New York, also known as the Twin Towers, causing the buildings to collapse and claim the lives of thousands of innocent workers, fire fighters, police officers, and other civilians.

    It was a destructive event that affected the lives of millions. People were sad, and devastated, for cherished loved ones had been murdered by hatred. Some citizens were outraged, angered by how our protectors could have ever let this have happened. American citizens were also scared, and feared the day, and asked themselves questions. "Why did it happen?" "Is it over, and if not, when will it stop?" "What happens now?" "Why is my loved one dead?" Or perhaps the most nerve-racking question of all, "Will it happen again, and if it does, who will it happen to?" So many other anguishing, frightful feelings and thoughts ran though the minds and the hearts of the country.

The evil event hurt me tremendously as an individual as well, not only because I am a peacemaker, but also because I have friends who were fire fighters who rushed into the World Trade Center to help save lives. Some of my brave fire fighter friends perished on that day. It is such an indescribably sad, angering, anguishing, and scary feeling to be sitting in front of the television, counting and searching for my friends on the scene, hoping and praying that they would not be harmed.

It was a truly sad day, but we must move on. It is OK to remember, to honor, and even to cry about the past as we move through this tragic anniversary. However, it is not OK to merely dwell in the tragedy of this anniversary. If we dwell in the past, we may ruin our future. By not being able to let go of fear and anger and pain, we may miss opportunities that open up in our lives, and offer us a step toward a better, and more peaceful future. It matters that we know "how some-thing happened," but it matters more to know "how we must respond" to events. It is our choice to pick the vision we use for inspiration and motivation, and to soften our hearts to see the good beyond any immediate situation.

We also must remember to always see the glass half full, and to never give up hope. September 11, 2001, was not just a day of terror; it was also the first day in a small time period when we, the people of the United States of America, bonded together. We did not bond as Democrat and Republican and Independent, or as Muslim and Jew and Christian and Hindu and Buddhist, or as black and white and Hispanic and Indian and Asian, or as foreign and native to this land. Rather, we bonded as Americans—as faithful patriots in politics and prayer. We recognized and respected true heroes, and helped support each other through a raging, terrible life-storm.

It is very sad that it took such a tragic event to make people unite so strongly. And it is also sad that the bond is fading already, even though we are only two years out in the anniversary of this event. War and cruel acts are never necessary, for they prove no real point, they solve no real problem, and they get real people nowhere. I pray that a horrible event such as September 11, 2001, never happens again, to this or any other nation. However, I also pray that one day, everybody in the entire world will come together, without the influence of a tragedy, and join hands. I pray that one day, we will collectively put our faith in each other, and in God by whatever name, and become one, without seeing differences in others as anything but beautiful and valuable. I pray that one day, we will achieve peace.

Amen.

Tele Vision

I kept my eyes
Open to the future.
Open and bright,
Never clouded with
Remnants of things
That just weren't right.
But 9/11 blew up
So very much dust
That we had to
Keep our eyes
Closed to the pain.
Closed and tight,
Ever shrouded with
Remains of those
Who just weren't the fight.

Now, together, let us
Close our eyes gently and
Bow our heads reverently,
Prayers on our lips,
Goodwill on our fingertips
Touching the world with
A meek and humble
Gesture of humanity.
And perhaps,
We can one day,
Open our eyes
To a gentle tomorrow.
We will keep our eyes
Open to the future.
Open and bright,
Never clouded or dusted with
Remnants of things or
Remains of those that
Just weren't right for a fight.

By Mattie J.T. Stepanek, July 17, 2002,
in *Reflections of a Peacemaker:
A Portrait Through Heartsongs*
(Andrews McMeel Publishing, 2005)

E-mail from: Jimmy Carter
Sent: March 18, 2003 6:42 AM EST
To: Mattie J.T. Stepanek
Subject: peace?

To Mattie: I'm looking forward to your being out of the hospital, and back at work with me on our peace project. With [the] beginning of what I consider to be an unjust and unnecessary war, all of us who are searching for peaceful solutions to problems need to work even harder. I've written a series of newspaper articles and have made speeches, but without success, and I'm really grieved today at the inevitable deaths of many innocent Iraqis and at least a small number of our superb American troops. I really need your ideas about what might be done. One or more of your poems would certainly be helpful. There have been a lot of discouraging times in my life, as well as yours, but we can prevail with faith and determination. I'm in the midst this week of a conference with Latin American leaders and will be lecturing at Emory University, but it would really be great if I could talk to you by telephone. I tried several times earlier, but was told that you could not take calls in the ICU. Now that you're doing better, I'll work with your mother on a convenient time.

With love, Jimmy Carter

E-mail from: Mattie J.T. Stepanek
Sent: Thursday, March 20, 2003 3:40 PM EST
To: Jimmy Carter
Subject: Re: peace?

Dear Jimmy,

Thank you for writing to me. I am hurting about the war, just like you. I cried last night when I saw the attack on Iraq. I am not trying to be disrespectful, but I feel like [the] decision [was made] long ago that [we were] going to have this war, and [people have] spent so much energy carving out the trench that would support [this] plan. Imagine if [they] had spent as much time and energy considering the possibility of peace as [they have] convincing others on the inevitability of war . . . we'd be at a different point in history today.

Look at the League of Nations. This country suggested it, but then didn't support it. And World War II was made possible. Look at the United Nations. This country suggested it. We have such huge input in the organization. And now, we are ignoring what it stands for. It was established to prevent war as much as possible. I am afraid that the UN will not survive any more than Iraq. And what happens after we "free" Iraq? Will we then boast triumph while that country's citizens struggle just as the citizens of Bosnia and Afghanistan and South Korea and how many other countries we have made "free" still struggle today? I don't understand. If [leaders like] Saddam [Hussein] and George W. [Bush] were kindergarteners, we could sit them down and talk this out. It's ridiculous how things are allowed to get out of hand. And look at the thirty countries that we list as supporting our efforts. They are mostly struggling countries, not countries that [are able to wait for and ensure] peace as it evolves, rather than fighting for it and demanding it.

I am very sad about it all. I am also glad, though, that I will try to help the situation with our book about peace. I think perhaps it should be called "Just Peace" since the word just has many denotations and connotations. I would like to make a list of the questions to be considered, and then a list of the people and peacemakers who might be interviewed. My publishers will try to see if they can get contact information for any of the people, and then I will send out letters. I am almost finished with my curriculum for this school year. The only thing I am behind in is Algebra II, and my research project. I am trying to do some [of the math] in the hospital, but it is so hard to concentrate.

I am more concerned about the research project because it was going to be something about the history of peacekeeping efforts and what might work or not work. Common sense tells me it's attitudes and people wanting things their own way, and whoever is stronger or more politically powerful dominates, at least for a while. But I need to do research and get facts and information. It seems that for as far back as history has been recorded, people have sought peace. But it also seems that people have given in to violence in the name of eventual peace. I want to look at patterns and see if we can break the cycle. Or at least make the circle of gentle peace seekers and peacemakers larger and stronger.

I need to go now, but I will write to you more. You said you wanted to call. It's not that I don't take calls, it's that I am in the Intensive Care Unit, so there's not usually a phone near me. Right now, though, I am in the Green ICU. The Blue ICU has no phones near the beds, but the Green ICU does. . . . So if you want to call you can, but I know you are very busy.

My mom thinks I am doing better. I am still bleeding and have some pain. Part of me wants to think I am getting better finally because for a while nobody was sure. But part of me is afraid it's just a good day instead of a real improvement. But I am getting plasma now, and Oprah asked people to pray. Prayer and Plasma. A great combination, don't you think? Blessed Miracles and Best Medicine can be the sequel! I love you a lot and I am sorry there is war in the world. You have worked so hard for peace, it just doesn't seem right. I will help you soon.

Love, Mattie

E-mail from: Jimmy Carter
Sent: Friday, March 21, 2003 8:01:44 AM EST
To: Mattie J.T. Stepanek
Subject: Re: peace?

To Mattie: You said you want to help me soon. You have already helped me with your beautiful message. I agree that plasma and prayer are a good combination, and we are certainly contributing our share of the prayers for your early recovery. Your indomitable will is another powerful factor.

I don't have any way to understand your physical limitations right now, but would like to suggest a strong and powerful poem, expressing concern about the unnecessary war, concern about the innocent children of Iraq, and hope for peace. I'm sure the *New York Times, Washington Post,* or *USA Today* would be glad to publish it and it would have a great impact on readers. I would be glad to help Jeni direct your words to the appropriate places if this seems to be an advisable project at this time. If not, maybe later when you're stronger.

Your love, wisdom, and insight really mean a lot to me.

Your friend, Jimmy Carter

Mattie in his trademark fishing hat, 2003.

The Rules of War

The rules of war have changed.
We've moved
From battlefields to backyards,
From arrows to anthrax,
From ninjas to nuclear weapons,
From swords to seron gas.
We used to
Fight for a just cause.
Now we
Fight, just because.
We used to win
Hand-to-hand,
Face-to-face.
Now we merely hear of
Children in mass graves
Mingled with the grown-ups
Who were protecting them
And their interests.
We are destroying everything
That we claim to be fighting for.
We can not win
Today's war with bombs.
We must resolve
Our issues with words.
The rules of war have changed.
How can we choose to continue
Playing this deadly
And impersonal game of loss?

By Mattie J.T. Stepanek, January 20, 2003,
in *Reflections of a Peacemaker: A Portrait Through Heartsongs*
(Andrews McMeel Publishing, 2005)

THE SAGES OF PEACE

When I was seven years old, I was assigned to write a report about any person, place, or thing that was of special interest to me. The teacher told the class that when something interested us, we should learn as much about it as possible. We were told that doing research would educate us about facts, and that facts are the basis of useful knowledge (rather than mere reports or even rumors by others) that would allow us to have well-considered opinions and to make well-informed decisions about many issues. I chose to study the life of a man named Jimmy Carter because he had been in some bit of news about a peacekeeping effort in another country, and the idea of "peace" mattered greatly to me. The lessons I learned from that assignment were invaluable for me as a student, and for my desire to become a peacemaker.

Through my research (see page 164), I became informed of many details about Carter's life and work, including the fact that he had, at some point in time, been a peanut farmer, a politician, a U.S. president, and a peacemaker. I learned that while serving as president, Carter worked diligently on peace efforts in the Middle East. Instead of simply vacationing at Camp David, the presidential retreat house, Carter would invite leaders of fighting countries to come and talk together in the mountains, and he would help mediate their issues. Also during his presidency, Carter became personally involved with Habitat for Humanity, an organization that helps people in need build their own homes, and he continues to be on the scene with a hammer and nails for ongoing projects. In the years after his presidency, he established the Carter Center, a private nonprofit organization where anyone and everyone can gather information about education, health, the environment, human rights, civil rights, and global conflict and mediation.

But I also learned about character and commitment in preparing this assignment, as I became aware of Carter's genuine humility, kindness, and love for all people. Through his example in all aspects of his life and work, I realized that it is OK to be proud of our goals and achievements as long as we choose a humble pride that roots us in our own reality, and not a vain pride that empties us of worthiness. The more I read and reflected on this individual who was now of great interest to me, the more I came to greatly admire the sincere dedication of Jimmy Carter to bringing about a just peace for our world as a whole. And, the more I read and reflected on issues of peace through my research on this man, the more I realized the imminent need for equity and peace on this earth, and for us to learn from role models, such as Jimmy Carter, as we plan peace and move into the future.

Several years later, when Carter was presented the Nobel Peace Prize in 2002, I knew many of the facts involved in the Nobel Committee's decision to recognize this man as the recipient of this laudable award. And, because of my research, I felt confident in my opinion that Jimmy Carter truly deserved the honor because of his consistent demonstration of patient understanding and supportive involvement with people and countries seeking to improve human and civil rights for all citizens. I knew that Carter's accomplishments in peacekeeping efforts, political disputes, and even the simple decisions of life, had made him one of the most respectable people in the world.

Across the years, I have continued researching and reflecting on the concept of peace, on people who seek peace, and on the different types of peace that are necessary. I have learned that peacemakers come in all ages, nationalities, ethnicities, professions, abilities, and aspirations. Some people seek inner peace for themselves and others, some people seek to establish peace within and between communities or countries, and some people seek to promote peace with the earth by advocating laws and practices that protect nature and the environment. Many advocates who choose to dedicate their lives to planning peace are members of internationally recognized organizations, and some advocates work toward peace within their own homes.

There are individuals who receive the Nobel Peace Prize in grand celebration for their efforts, and there are children and adults whose personal dedication and accomplishments toward world peace will never be acknowledged publicly. But all who are committed to seeking, planning, and realizing the justness of peace share a strong spirit of gentle bravery and respect for the gifts of life. And every finger dabbed into the waters of hope has the same opportunity to ripple into the collective waves of peace, touching possibility to reality.

People who choose to embrace peace often have to battle as they advocate for the basic needs and rights of others. However, peacemakers draw on nonviolent methods of battle, such as collaborative discussion rather than conquering devastation. Throughout history there have been many organizations and individuals role modeling the effectiveness of mediation, negotiation, redistribution, boycotts, picketing, petitions, letter writing, political cartoons, even dramatic portrayals in song and dance and story, as a means of both conflict resolution and societal campaigning and education about the need for peace and equity.

In striving for a just peace—for ourselves, for our communities, for our world—it is important to recognize and consider the efforts of others, past and present. Who are the role models that we can look to for direction? There are so many organizations and individuals working toward justice and peace at so many different levels. As we consider the future and efforts toward planning peace, it is essential to understand the past and to reflect on the reality of the present, so that we are truly informed and ready to step into each next moment in a way that allows and provides for equity among all the world.

ORGANIZATIONS FOR PEACE

Perhaps the most unified and successful effort for organized world peace was the creation of the United Nations (UN) on October 24, 1945. World War II was still raging, but world leaders recognized the need for a well-respected assembly of nations that would provide mediation and other nonviolent methods of resolving conflicts and disputes between countries. The UN actually grew out of a well-intended, but short-lived and unsuccessful attempt for world peace through the League of Nations, which was formulated at the end of World War I. Woodrow Wilson, who was the U.S. president at the time, enthusiastically supported the concept and development of the League of Nations to prevent another world war, and was committed to this country becoming an active member of the organization. However, the U.S. Senate would not allow President Wilson to sign the treaty, which would enter our country into an official alliance with other nations.

There are different opinions about why the U.S. Senate did not support the League of Nations, but the most common deduction is that the decision was based on the feeling at that time that this country should isolate, or somehow separate, itself from problems that existed and would continue to arise in other countries around the world. People had just witnessed the devastation of the world at war, and many U.S. citizens were hesitant to be a part of world issues and tribulations that might bring the country into another war of the world. Without the United States, which has long been one of the most powerful countries in the world, the League of Nations was an ineffective assembly, and was unable to stop the smaller fights and the tyranny that led to World War II.

As the second "war to end all wars" raged on, the citizens and leaders of the United States and other allied countries realized that the lessons of noncommitment to an organized peace effort could not be disregarded. Representatives from the United States met with representatives from Great Britain, China, and what was at the time the Soviet Union, and agreed to establish an international peacekeeping organization. U.S. President Franklin Delano Roosevelt suggested that it be called the United Nations, and a short time later, men and women from forty-six different countries gathered to draft the charter for this organization. Today, 191 independent countries are members of the United Nations. These countries are large and small, and the represented citizens are people of all races and cultures and religions and economic situations.

Even though the UN represents billions and billions of people around the world, it is not a "superpower." Power is shared among all the countries who have joined the UN, and the delegate of each nation gets one vote on each issue, no matter how large or small their nation is in territory or population or resources. In a balanced approach, the UN seeks equitable resolutions that prevent war and maintain world peace and security. The UN also works to develop friendships among all nations, and to promote social justice so that all people in the world can live a good life.

With input, advice, and mediation from the UN, our world has been spared from many potential wars. The UN, and other organizations involved directly with the UN, have been recognized with the Nobel Peace Prize on many occasions for their enduring commitment to and powerful impact on ensuring provisions of equity and security to all citizens of Earth. Yet, the UN is sometimes not effective in preventing war, when too many people in a group see violence as a quick means to an end, or when one country chooses not to listen to the recommendations and sanctions of the UN. And, there are conflicts within the UN. For example, a few decades ago, the organization refused to allow China, a founding member of the organization, in the General Assembly because it is a communist country, which is considered by many to be a threat to world freedom, independence, and equity.

Opinions vary on the justness of this decision. We could choose to risk the inclusion of China, because it is such a large nation and could bring much power to the effort of peace. But we could also be concerned that even though each nation has just one vote regardless of size, the presence of a communist country could lead to the use of propaganda and political power to try and persuade other countries to vote in favor of communism or violence. We could wonder whether a communist country might use the UN as a means of spying on efforts toward world peace and safety. But we could also wonder whether a communist country might gain new insights on justice and world peace by witnessing and being an essential part of the world body responsible for peacekeeping efforts.

The members of the UN work to achieve human and civil rights and to support and provide for the basic needs of all people, and they try to help people suffering from intolerance that often leads to brutality, such as cultural or religious oppression. The UN also supports the environment, by protecting all kinds of nature, including animals, land, water, and air, and it provides help to people and countries during environmental disasters such as hurricanes, earthquakes, floods, and droughts. The organization provides health care, medicine, and food to people in need, and seeks to fight and eradicate diseases that too often kill people, especially those people living in vulnerable and poor countries where lifesaving immunizations and treatments are not readily available. The UN even supports space study, which may lead to solutions in medicine and other essential research areas.

So often we hear the phrase "children are the future." It sounds cliché, but it is true. The leaders of our world were once children. And the children of the world will one day be the leaders, or the adults and parents of more children represented by the leaders. The UN recognizes that children are an important part of the world, and of the decisions being made that shape the future of the world. The UN represents children of all nations, and tries to help children achieve the safest, healthiest, and best future possible. And, the UN nurtures the growing voices and input of children from countries around the world by supporting educational programs, schools, and camps, in which children attend, study, and speak about world issues. The world leaders of today are already hearing the voice of children as they consider the essential issues of the future, including health, safety, security, human rights, and peace.

INDIVIDUALS FOR PEACE

In the early 1900s, Mahatma Gandhi, a man from India, helped people in South Africa fight against unfair laws in that country. There was no brutality during the fight, though, because Gandhi was a pacifist who believed in the use of nonviolent techniques to wage a battle. Some years later, Gandhi helped the people of his own country fight for freedom from oppression. Again, using nonviolent protest, he changed the course of his nation and inspired others with statements like, "An eye for an eye will make the whole world blind."

During the middle of the twentieth century, Martin Luther King Jr. fought against racial segregation and prejudice in the United States. Like Gandhi, King believed that the fight for human and civil rights need not involve bloodshed, and that equity should and could be achieved through protest, demonstration, and other nonviolent methods of conflict resolution. In one of his many speeches King said, "The nonviolent resister not only refuses to shoot his opponent, but he also refuses to hate him." King, who said he spoke as "a citizen of the world," was awarded the Nobel Peace Prize in 1964 for his use of nonviolent methods to change laws that violated human and civil rights.

Gandhi and King are just two examples of individuals who have long been recognized as powerful and effective change agents, and who are both well-respected for their achievements as peace activists. There are many other individuals who have also worked hard—even risked their jobs and lives—in the effort to seek, promote, and ensure peace for individuals and for all nations.

Marian Wright Edelman is currently a strong advocate for justice, and speaks out strongly for the needs and rights of children. In seeking to protect the rights of children, Edelman is also advocating for the future. Children are the future, according to Edelman, and adults must recognize that children learn from them, the present. Edelman believes that if children have basic needs met, like their need for food, water, health care, education, safety, and a clean environment in which to live, they can grow up better and not feel the need to fight other people. It would be important for us to know more about Edelman's thoughts on how we could and should serve as peaceful role models for children, for the future, because we must consider the reality that when people are able to feel good about who they are as a person, they are better able to help other people feel good about who they are too, which is essential to a just peace.

Some people do not plan to make a positive difference in the world. But some tragedy happens in their life, or in the life of a family member or friend, or even just in the life of someone they learn about through the news. They find themselves in a position where they can somehow be a source of inspiration, a source of strength, a source of resources, or even a source of security, for others who are in need.

Elie Wiesel witnessed the catastrophic events of World War II from the inside of a Jewish concentration camp. After his horrific experience, during which he watched the terror of war lead to the deaths of his own family members and friends, he wrote essays and books recounting his ordeal, and how he survived both physically and spiritually. From Wiesel's experiences and reflections, we can learn important lessons, such as not losing faith in oneself and in other human beings and even in one's God, no matter how hopeless and helpless a situation may seem. Wiesel, who received the

Nobel Peace Prize in 1986 for his humanitarian efforts in response to the Holocaust, also teaches us, like many other peacemakers, about integrating reactions to the past with the need for peaceful attitudes in the present. He has said that although it is natural to be upset and angry about inequities and injustices of the past, we should never hold grudges or dwell in the past or we may become blind to opportunities for the present and the future.

Other ordinary citizens who make a commitment to being a part of world peace may never be publicly acknowledged. My friend Ron Wyatt worked as a police sergeant in Washington, D.C., for many years. But in 1999, he chose to spend time training to be a part of the United Nations peacekeeping effort in the country of Kosovo. He made a commitment to leave his wife and seven-year-old daughter for an entire year, so that he could share his professional skills by serving as an International Police Monitor. In doing so, Wyatt would be providing basic law enforcement for the country of Kosovo, and training, evaluating, and monitoring other people as the United Nations created a fair police force in this war-torn country.

Initially, Wyatt said he thought he would be training to serve in East Timor. However, the UN sent Wyatt (and about 450 other citizens from countries like Canada, France, Germany, Italy, Pakistan, Thailand, and the United States) to Kosovo because at that time, this was a country that needed much support, monitoring, and assistance. Wyatt told me that he was not looking forward to being separated from his family by such a great distance and for such a long period, and that his family was very concerned about his safety and well-being in a country struggling to seek peace, but still filled with violence, often against the people who enter to serve as peacekeepers. But he also said that he was committed to supporting efforts toward world peace and justice, and he felt it was important "to accept this opportunity to share skills in an ongoing attempt to bring order and security to a place where many people have suffered a great deal."

We can also gain valuable lessons by learning from people who are directly affected by poverty and violence and discrimination. Imagine the collective understanding and compassion we could cultivate by sitting down and listening to the thoughts and words and experiences of mothers who cannot find health care or immunizations for their babies, or fathers who cannot find work or food or water for their families, or teenagers who are obligated into military service to seek an end to injustice. Imagine the days and nights, and the descriptions and dreams, of children who know of no other life than one filled with the fear of more explosions or pain or hunger or captivity or thirst or slavery or violence or mockery or invasion or destruction or death. It is painful for me to imagine such devastation in my life, or in the lives of people I know and love. But it is happening every day in life, to people who need to be known, and loved, by others who care, and who are willing to listen and then make a difference.

LESSONS FOR PEACE

When we look back in history, and when we look around at the world today, it is clear that many organizations and individuals desire peace, and try different approaches to seek a solution to the sad reality of inequity and of violence and war. And in retrospect, we can judge the intentions and outcomes of various ideas and endeavors as being successful or as being failures. Clearly, some plans for securing justice work, and some plans do not work as well, or do not work at all.

At first glance, the Nobel Peace Prize would seem simply to be a coveted and noble honor created by some group of people to recognize other groups of people who have demonstrated outstanding commitment and efforts in some area of world peace. Actually, the award was created when Alfred Nobel, a Swedish chemist who had invented dynamite, died. Nobel assumed that when people around the world became aware of the destructive powers of his invention, they would be careful not to use it in a way that would hurt people. He hoped that it would only be used in construction. Unfortunately, countries starting buying dynamite from him and using it as a weapon of violence, and war, as they fought for particular rights or desires.

Nobel thought that a solution to the situation would be to make sure every country had some amount of dynamite. He reasoned that this way, each country would fear the potential power of destruction from every other country, and, therefore, no war would be declared because no country would want the retaliation of dynamite used in their homeland, or on their own citizens. Nobel's intentions may have been noble, but they backfired. Instead of eliminating the threat of war by selling so much dynamite, countries bought more and more dynamite so that they could wage bigger and bigger wars.

Nobel became very rich from the sales, but he also came to realize that we cannot achieve peace through fear, horror, intimidation, and the threatening power of violent weapons. When he died, instead of leaving his fortune to his family and friends, Nobel used the money to establish five annual awards. Four of the five awards would go to chemists or other scientists making remarkable advances and discoveries that help people live better lives. The fifth award, the Nobel Peace Prize, would go to organizations or individuals exemplifying efforts toward world peace. Today, the Nobel Peace Prize consists of a large sum of money and a medal, given to great peacemakers in the world.

Some ideas for peace bring equitable results, but some need more thought and planning. Some changes in our world are for the better, but some are not. Some people say that there has been more progress toward justice and peace in the world with the existence of the UN than during the previous millennia when there was no international peacekeeping organization. And it is true that many more people today have food, water, health care, and a safe place to live than in the past. What the organizations like the UN and individuals like Jimmy Carter have done is very impressive. But the world still has lots of problems and we have a long way to go in planning a just peace for all citizens of the world.

Organizations and individuals have made a remarkable difference in creating a healthier and more peaceful world in many areas. And we can gain insight and practical knowledge by being open to the thoughts, words, and experiences of others who have already endeavored to plan peace. There are lessons to be learned from successful endeavors, there are lessons to be learned from concepts that did not work, and there are lessons to be learned from the people who are in the desperate situations of poverty and war and other injustices.

Indeed, there is still much to learn and to do as we consider a real plan for justice and peace that reaches all people. Issues that have long been sources of conflict, like racism and religious oppression, still exist within and between countries. There are still millions and millions of people whose basic needs are not being met. Because they do not have access to enough water, food, health care, education, or a safe place to live, there are millions of people who are thirsty, and who are starving, and who do not have a future, and who are homeless, and who are victims of violence, and who are dying from illnesses and diseases that are often treatable or eradicated in other areas of the world. And worst of all, individuals and groups of people are still fighting over little things. We are still choosing to hurt and retaliate and threaten each other, in our efforts to satisfy our own needs, and desires.

Since I was very young, my mother has taught me a valuable lesson. She says: "You are not at the center of the universe. The world does not revolve around you, nor does it revolve around me. But, you and I are essential to the balance of the revolving world. We are each essential creations in the circle of life." How true. How wise. I, like every person ever created, am a unique being, with some gift for the world. And going around and around with so many other people in so many other countries, each of us trying to balance our own needs and rights and desires with those of every other person is a great challenge. But it is a challenge that I believe calls to each of us. And it is a challenge that I believe we can answer with the statement, "Peace is possible, if we make it something that really matters." If we choose to make peace an attitude and a habit, then a just peace will become a reality.

Mattie taking time to rest and reflect with his service dog, Micah, February 2003.

E-mail from: Nancy Hunt, President, WAFF
Date: July 1, 2002
To: Mattie Stepanek
Subject: Copy of my letter posted on the WAFF Web site

Mattie Stepanek is an eleven-year-old (soon to be twelve) boy, a poet, and a peace-maker. Since birth, Mattie has been fighting dysautonomic mitochondrial myopathy, a rare and fatal form of muscular dystrophy that weakens the muscles in his body. (From CNN's *Larry King Live,* April 2002)

The We Are Family Foundation was just being formed during early spring 2002, to promote diversity, understanding, respect, and the vision of a global family. The WAFF project began in response to the tragic events of September 11th. Legendary songwriter/producer Nile Rodgers and Tommy Boy Music president Tom Silverman gathered 200 celebrities on the weekend of September 22, 2001, to rerecord Nile's world-renowned hit song "We Are Family" to commence the healing process. The recording sessions that weekend again proved the song's power to give hope and allow people to feel better through an uplifting beat and a message of unity. The event was captured on film as a documentary by director Danny Schechter entitled *The Making and Meaning of "We Are Family"* and a music video by director Spike Lee.

The power of the We Are Family Project continued. Rodgers and Christopher Cerf, award-winning children's TV/music producer, next called together over 100 beloved characters from the world of children's television for the first time in history and recorded a children's version of the song. The music video aired as a public service announcement simultaneously on the Disney Channel, Nickelodeon, and PBS on March 11, 2002, with a unified message of the importance of a global family.

Nile had no idea that the hit song he and his late music partner, Bernard Edwards, wrote for Sister Sledge in 1979 would be a part of history again by helping to bring people together and give hope that we can live together in a peaceful world. But there we were, having our inaugural board of directors meeting after receiving nonprofit status, and talking about having our first fund-raiser to really launch the organization. One of our board members, Mark Barondess, suggested that we present an award to someone at the fund-raiser. I had not thought about that before— what kind of an award would we give, who would we give it to, and for what?

For the next few days this idea of an award stuck in the back of my head with the same questions—who, what, why? Then, one night I was flipping channels and stopped for more than a moment at *Larry King Live* on CNN. There was a child speaking as an adult, how could that be? I have heard and seen child geniuses before, but this boy was beyond anything I had ever encountered. As I listened to him recite his poetry I became more and more mesmerized by his words, wisdom, and level of understanding of our humanity. It was the first time that I had actually seen Larry King with a look of complete amazement, astonishment, and awe all in the same expression. And, he wasn't alone as I am sure my facial expressions and the rest of his audience's that night were identical.

The boy's name is Mattie—Mattie J.T. Stepanek. He is eleven. He has a rare form of MD. He has three siblings who already died from the same disease. And, he is a messenger to our humanity. Mattie is a poet, a peacemaker, and a spirit of hope and enlightenment. He is the We Are Family Foundation's first honoree and the award is called the We Are Family Peacemaker Award. In one fell swoop I knew the answers to the "who, what, and why" that I had been struggling with for days. At 10:00 p.m., immediately after *Larry King Live,* I called our board member who suggested the idea of the award and who also happens to represent Larry King. I said, "Mark, I just found our honoree on Larry King and we are calling our award the We Are Family Peacemaker Award. Get me Larry's producer and find Mattie!" I waited until midnight to call Nile who was in England (six hours ahead) and told him about Mattie. Mark and Nile were both thrilled with my excitement, but it was not until they read Mattie's best-selling poetry books that they truly understood my ecstatic behavior.

Later I found out from Mark that not only was Mattie Larry King's favorite interview in his forty-five year career, but that he spent an entire hour reciting Mattie's poetry to his wife, Shawn, later on his plane. I also found out that Mattie lives in Maryland with his mother, Jeni, who also has MD, and that this was only about twenty miles from the location of our first fund-raiser. Fate had intervened. Mattie and Jeni would be able to attend our event and receive the award without any transportation problems—they can drive their new custom van that Oprah purchased for them to meet their medical and physical needs!

On June 24, 2002, Nile, Mark, and I met Mattie and Jeni. Needless to say our lives were changed forever by the innocence, wisdom, and purity that we encountered that day. I hope that you experience the same transformation as we did by reading his books and learning about this special boy and his mother who has never given up on life or her children.

Mattie, his mom, Jeni, and his service dog, Micah, with Larry King after one of Mattie's many interviews with the talk show host.

Mattie and Nile Rodgers pretend to be gargoyles during a break from the planning session for the We Are Family Foundation Inaugural Gala in Annapolis, Maryland, June 2002.

Mattie sharing his poem "For Our World" at the inaugural We Are Family Foundation Gala in Annapolis, Maryland, July 2002. It was Mattie's hope that this poem would serve as an "international poem for peace."

Mattie talking about his "message of hope and peace" with Shawn King during the inaugural fund-raising gala for the We Are Family Foundation in Annapolis, Maryland, July 2002.

(Right and below) Mattie receiving the first We Are Family Peacemaker Award during the inaugural fund-raising gala for the organization, July 2002. On stage with him are musician and WAFF founder Nile Rodgers, talk show host Montel Williams, and Shawn King, the wife of talk show host Larry King.

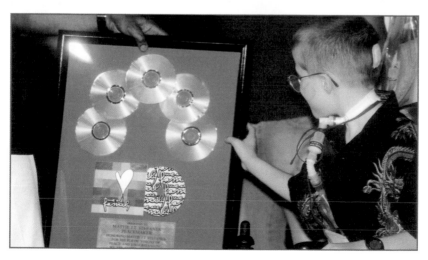

Mattie doing his "Larry King impression" while waiting to be interviewed by the talk show host, April 2002.

Mattie with Larry King and Washington Redskins owner Dan Snyder, during one of Mattie's last public events, March 5, 2004. Three days later, Mattie went into heart failure; he died later that year on June 22.

Mattie with musician and WAFF founder Nile Rodgers, and his mom, Jeni, during the Larry King Cardiac Foundation fund-raiser in Washington, D.C., March 2004.

Mattie talks with poet Maya Angelou during a book signing in College Park, Maryland, April 2002.

(Above) Mattie's mom, Jeni, presents Maya Angelou the newly renamed WAFF Mattie J.T. Stepanek Peacemaker Award during the foundation's New York gala, April 2005.

(Left) A "movie ticket" in Mattie's honor issued at Children's National Medical Center in Washington, D.C., the hospital where Mattie spent most of his final years. The WAFF, with the Lollipop Theater Network, now sponsors "Mattie's Movie and Poetry Day" at several children's hospitals.

On Being a Champion

A champion is a winner,
A hero . . .
Someone who never gives up
Even when the going gets rough.
A champion is a member of
A winning team . . .
Someone who overcomes challenges
Even when it requires creative solutions.
A champion is an optimist,
A hopeful spirit . . .
Someone who plays the game,
Even when the game is called life . . .
Especially when the game is called life.
There can be a champion in each of us,
If we live as a winner,
If we live as a member of the team,
If we live with a hopeful spirit,
For life.

By Mattie J.T. Stepanek,
September 13, 1999,
in *Journey Through Heartsongs*
(Hyperion/VSP, 2002)

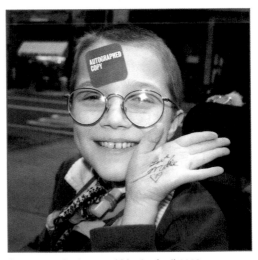

An autographed copy of Mattie, April 2002.

E-mail from: Mattie J.T. Stepanek
Sent: May 19, 2003 7:35 AM EST
To: Jimmy Carter
Subject: (no subject)

Dear Jimmy,

Hi. It's me, Mattie. I just wanted to tell you that I am still in the ICU, but "I" am still here! It's been a rough few months. But things are going to be OK. I am still bleeding a lot from my trachea and my lips and some of my fingers. And there are many things wrong with my body. But, I am going to go home on Sunday of Memorial Day weekend I think. It's exciting but also scary because I am not going home because I am better. I am going home because it is time. It is time to live again, before whatever is going to happen to my body finishes happening. I will have to come back to the hospital every other day for platelet transfusions and every week for red blood, and I need lots of IV fluids to keep my blood pressure up, but I am still here, and I have decided that it is time for me to get back to work on my message. And could you please tell Mrs. Carter that I am ready to talk with her or her staff about our conference on intergenerational caregiving this summer. I am very excited about being an ambassador for that. I want to be a peacemaker and a daddy. And being an "ambassador" is being a "peacemaker" if the role is used correctly. I am a little bit sad and scared about going home since nobody knows what is going to happen next, or when, to me. But I am mostly very excited. I will get to do my MDA work, and I will do some book signings (I hope), and I will get back to work on the "Just Peace" book project that you were helping me with. I have made a list of possible questions and people to interview that I would like to share with you sometime. But first I need to do some more research on the history of peace-making so I make sure I am asking the right questions and understanding the input of world leaders. Oh, I forgot to ask you if you have heard Billy Gilman's new CD. It's called *Music Through Heartsongs: Songs Based on the Poems of Mattie J.T. Stepanek.* He's listed as "country" but it's not a country album. It's a mix of spiritual and soft rock and Caribbean and Hawaiian and country. But mostly, it's a strong, gentle, convincing voice singing my message of hope and peace. I think you would really like the very first song, "For Our World," because it is a song of peace for the world. The fourth song, "I AM/Shades of Life" was made into a really cool music video, that uses my "mosaic of life" idea. Each person and part of nature is a part of a mosaic . . . We can scatter the pieces or we can gather them to create something meaningful . . . It has a surprise ending, so I won't tell you about it. Well, I need to go, but I wanted to tell you that I love you, and that I strive to be like you. When I want to give up, I think about you, and the struggles you have had and how you don't give up. You dream big. You live big. And so, you touch the world big. That's what I want to do. Tell your family I said hello, please.

Love, Mattie

E-mail from: Jimmy Carter
Sent: May 24, 2003 10:02 AM EST
To: Mattie J.T. Stepanek
Subject: (no subject)

Mattie: We have just returned from the West Coast after a full week of promoting the Carter Center, and received your very beautiful and encouraging message—five days after you sent it and the day before you're planning to leave ICU. We are delighted that you will be going home, and will be praying extra hard that liberation from the hospital will be good for you, both physically and emotionally. I'm not surprised to learn that your ambition to promote peace and love has been a strong driving factor in your decision to make this change. Rosalynn has the message also, and I'm sure she will be responding, perhaps directly with your mom.

It's hard to imagine how Billy Gilman could improve on the impact of your poems with music, but we'll be getting a copy of the CD for a new dose of inspiration, which all of us need on occasion. I hope you realize that you are continuing every day to have a profound impact on the conscience and ideals of millions of people with the work you have already done, so you must not feel guilty during the days when you have to receive treatment and care from your mom and the doctors. There is no way to describe how proud I am of you, and how much I value your friendship and our shared beliefs in a more peaceful and loving world. When I'm discouraged or confused, I'm strengthened by your courage and insights.

Just send an e-mail any time, or place a call to [the Carter Center]. [They] always know how to reach me if I happen to be traveling.

Love, Jimmy

E-mail from: Jimmy Carter
Date: July 13, 2003 8:33 AM EST
To: Mattie J.T. Stepanek
Subject: Thanks

Mattie: I am delighted with your almost miraculous improvement, obviously the result of your resilience and courage, the care of your mother and the doctors, and the prayers of a multitude of those who love you. Rosalynn was thrilled to have you as a partner in the recent events in Washington, and she will be writing to thank you personally. She brought home your poetry and the clock, with your remarkable marking of the hours with reminders of your basic philosophy. Thank you, very much.

As usual, we continue our work at the Carter Center and are making good progress. We've been involved in Liberia for many years, and I've been encouraging the Bush administration to give some modest support there. I have an article in the *New York Times* this morning on the subject. During my spare time I am trying to improve my skills in painting, with oils and acrylics. It's a hobby that I can continue after age restricts some other activities. I wonder if you've ever had much interest in the visual arts.

Best wishes, and love from Jimmy Carter

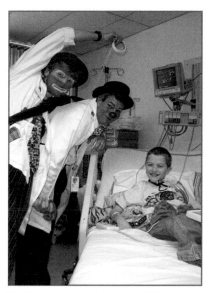

Mattie enjoys a visit from the "Clown Care Unit" during a four-month stay in the Pediatric Intensive Care Unit at Washington, D.C., Children's National Medical Center, March 2003.

Mattie with his service dog, Micah, at the February 2004 Heartsongs Gala in Washington, D.C.

The Church Ride

Sometimes,
I think that there should be a very special
Carnival ride, that is all about church.
All of the people will go inside
The church and sit in the pews.
We will hear a voice on the loudspeaker
That will say, "Buckle your seat belts."
After everyone buckles up,
We will hear a loud boom-click,
And the doors will be shut tight,
And lock us in from the outside.
And then the voice will say,
"Your journey is about to begin."
And the church will rise up
And spin and zoom and whirl all around . . .
And everyone will not know for sure
Whether they are excited, or scared.
And suddenly,
We will see light all around,
And Angels singing "Alleluia!"
And we will feel so happy and good,
And there will be nothing that we want.
The voice on the loud speaker will say,
"This is Heaven, folks. Heaven is a wonderful place!"
And the people on the ride will sing
"Alleluia" with the Angels,
And with the each-other people on the ride,
And with the people in Heaven
Who we used to know when they were alive.

But then,

The church will start to spin and zoom and whirl

All around again, and it will get so windy and dark . . .

And windy and dark, and the

Light of the Angels will disappear.

And we will look out and see all of the devils,

And we will be sad and afraid.

The devils will be laughing like the Angels,

But it will be mean and nasty laughing without any "Alleluias."

And we will all scream out, "Help us! Help us!

How do we get back to life? Help us!"

And the voice on the loudspeaker will say,

"Follow the good. Follow the good people,

And follow the good light,

And follow the good laughing sounds.

Do not follow the bad, even if you hear laughing.

It is not happy laughing.

It is your choice, but to get back to life,

Follow the good, people, follow the good!"

And the Church Ride will begin

To go back down to Earth . . .

And it will land safely where it began.

The seat belts will unbuckle,

The doors will unlock,

And the voice on the loudspeaker will say,

"Welcome back. I hope you have enjoyed your journey.

Do not forget this ride, ever.

Goodbye, and have a good life."

And we will each leave the Church Ride,

And go through the doors, to make our choice.

By Mattie J.T. Stepanek, June 4, 1995, in *Reflections of a Peacemaker:
A Portrait Through Heartsongs* (Andrews McMeel Publishing, 2005)

Opportunity Knocking

I open the door
To each new day.
I welcome the dawn and
I swing open wide
The entry portal
To each next moment in life.
Some days thrust tsunamis
With storms and squalls.
Some days shower sunshine
With laughter and love.
Some days illustrate
The circle of life,
Highlighting the grass which
Is always greener
On the other side of the hills
Where blossoms grow and
The land prospers
Fruitfully and the
Dreams always come true,
Or perhaps,

They don't really
Stand a chance.
As birds announce life
Through sweet or sad songs
Of that part of the circle
Which cannot be seen
From this side,
I walk with content
In the green of my youth
Though shaded with challenges
Each darkened or lightened by
My choices in vision and views.
But I know that if only
I open my eyes and
I open my mind and
I open my life then
I open the door
To each new day.

By Mattie J.T. Stepanek, April 7, 2002,
in *Reflections of a Peacemaker:
A Portrait Through Heartsongs*
(Andrews McMeel Publishing, 2005)

Rebuilding the Mosaic

Hope is not passive,
It's real and alive,
Hope is a strength
To guide choices made wise.

Excerpt from "About Hope," May 21, 2003,
by Mattie J.T. Stepanek, in *Reflections of a Peacemaker:
A Portrait Through Heartsongs*
(Andrews McMeel Publishing, 2005)

Believing in Someday

Maybe,
Someday,
We will all join hands
And live together . . .
Helping each other,
Loving each other.
Maybe,
Someday,
We will all make the world
A much better place . . .
And be like a gigantic,
Smoothly rushing river of peace—
A loving circle that nothing can break.
Maybe,
Someday,
We may start with just one person,
And one permanent peace agreement
Within one's self, within one's world.
Personal peace can then spread
Within and between the families,
Then within and between communities,
And then within and around the whole world.
Maybe,
Someday,
We can become
As close to perfect
As anything and anyone can get.
Let us each join our own Heartsong
With this old song of the heart, and believe . . .
"Let there be peace on earth,
And let it begin with me."

By Mattie J.T. Stepanek, August 20, 2000,
in *Hope Through Heartsongs*
(Hyperion/VSP, 2002)

E-mail From: Mattie J.T. Stepanek
Sent: December 05, 2003 7:25 PM EST
To: Sandy Newcomb
Subject: Faith/religion conversation

Dear Sandy,

Thank you for inviting me to help out at your church last week. I love working with children, and it meant a lot to me to have the opportunity to sign "Silent Night." When I use sign language it always makes me think of my brother Jamie, because that was how we communicated. I am glad that I am welcomed by your community, even though I am a member of a different religion. That's how the whole world should be . . . welcoming. I know that what we believe in matters to each of us, but like we were talking about last week, I believe that religion should be a structural framework to strengthen faith, rather than an organized force to divide, or even conquer, in the name of faith. I did a lot of journaling about this whole issue, and wanted to share some of my thoughts with you that grew from our conversation last week.

I believe that there is a supreme being or force that created everything and everyone. I also believe in the proofs of science and in the concepts of evolution. I do not believe that faith and science must be in conflict, or oppose each other. I believe that they are actually complementary. But surely, something, some essence and energy, has been ever-present, and will continue to be ever-present, through-out all of history. Though there are many options for explaining this, I choose to call that one great existence, through both faith and science, God.

I also believe that we have all been granted the gift of free will, and that we should all be free to choose how, and even if, we pray to a supreme being. We should be free to choose the name we use to refer to our creator, and we should be free to choose whether and which religion guides our spirituality. But I firmly believe that we should never use our religion, our faith, our spirituality, or even our choice of nonbelieving, as a reason or basis to diminish the freedom or rights or faith of another person.

I believe that people are good, although we sometimes do not make choices that are good in nature, or choices that are for the good of all. And, I believe that God, by all names and beliefs, is good. No God uses gifts of creation as pawns to destroy other gifts of creation. And no God imposes suffering on individuals or groups at the request of any other individual or group. Some suffering occurs because of the natural course of natural events. Other suffering, especially inflicted suffering, occurs because of choices of people. It is all wrapped up in our gift of free will, and is not because God wills suffering or chooses sides in a conflict. Otherwise, all of creation would be mere puppetry in the scheme of life. This is not so. And because suffering naturally exists, I cannot understand why we, as good

humans, would ever choose to inflict additional physical or mental or spiritual suffering on any other human.

Particularly now, during the December holiday season, the news is filled with
details of lawsuits and allegations of bias and infringement and whatever because
of simple intolerance. Because of narrow-mindedness and even self-righteousness.
Seeing or hearing or witnessing the name, rituals, or tenets of any religion should
not be deemed as offensive. If I say, "I have chosen to believe that Jesus is my
Savior, Lord, and God," I am not saying that anyone else must believe the same
thing. If I have chosen to be a Roman Catholic, because I truly believe in the
Eucharist, and in the concept of ordinary people becoming saints to serve as role
models and inspiration and intercessors during difficult times in life, I am not
implying that all Christians must think or worship like me.

Likewise, when I see a menorah lit up in a public place, I do not feel that
someone is trying to persuade me to think or pray in a given way. Nor do I feel that
someone is trying to offend me by not displaying an emblem of my own beliefs. I
merely see an icon of expression, a religious image, reminding me of the diverse
and unique aspects in the treasured mosaic of life. In reality, no living person can
have absolute and certain knowledge about which religion may or may not be
absolutely accurate. Faith cannot be proven. Faith merely guides us, inspires us,
and the structured rituals of a particular faith should serve as a support during
crises, pain, and difficult times in life, not as a battle cry.

Although I am a Catholic Christian, I have tried to read about other religions,
because I believe that when we know about something, we can better understand
it. And when we understand something, there is less fear and misunderstanding,
which often comes from uncertainty. And in all the religious doctrine and material
that I have read for and by Christians, Jews, Muslims, Buddhists, Hindus, and others, I have never found a statement in which God, by whatever name, asks people
to kill or rule other people in that name. Nor have I found any religious doctrine
that says we are not to tolerate different approaches to goodness and justness. I
have found many interpretations made by humans, though, whereby an assump-
tion is made that one religion should dominate or smite another. But then, long has
it been known though that "to err is human."

There are words and passages in many books about God's wrath and desire,
and about humans begging Yahweh or Allah or Jesus to assist them in their personal and societal battles. But in all the doctrine and scripture on which particular
religions are based, or at least in all that I have been able to read, I have only
found a peaceful and generous and available supreme being, whose common
command is rooted in spiritual love and respect. I believe that God, by whatever
name and faith, is present, even active, in our world, but not controlling. As one
army calls out God's name during the raging battle, do we not think that the other
side is calling out God's name as well? The baby who dies of a disease, the woman

who suffers brain damage in a car accident, the man who perishes in war, are no less valued or touched by the reality and presence of God in their lives than those who miraculously survive.

It is humans who claim "there but for the grace of God go I." It is humans that make the decision to try and use, or claim, the power of a supreme being in taking sides of a battlefield. The violence chronicled in battles of the past, and the prophetic violence captured in word for the future, represent human reasoning and interpretation based on our own physical and spiritual needs, and fears. We should never take our freedom to choose the name of God as a means to infringe on the rights and desires of others and their freedoms. And we should never allow our religious structure to divide us from others, our brothers and sisters in the name of scientific or faithful creation.

Well, I have to go now, but I just wanted to thank you for including me, and I wanted to thank your community for welcoming me. I am having a rough time now medically, which is difficult for my mind and spirit as well as my body, and some-times makes it a challenge to be positive and happy and feel good about life. Thank you for spending time with me, for talking with me, for making me smile, and for making a difference to me so that I can continue to try and make a differ-ence for others. I love you.

Love, your VFKBF ("very favorite kid best friend"), Mattie

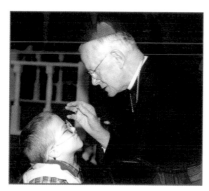

Mattie with Cardinal James A. Hickey during the Jubilee 2000 celebration in Washington, D.C.

Mattie translating "Silent Night" into sign language as his mom, Jeni, sings with the Holy Rosary Family Choir in Upper Marlboro, Maryland, December 1998.

E-mail from: Mattie J.T. Stepanek
Sent: January 06, 2004 2:09 PM EST
To: Jeni Stepanek
Subject: We Need to Dream

My ideas for an essay that would recognize the lasting impact of Martin Luther King Jr. on the national holiday commemorating his noble work:

To begin, I will provide a brief overview of the reality of racism, including definitions and examples from the past and the present. As this section develops, I will briefly review King's life, including who he was as a person, what he stated to be his dream, and why his dream mattered so much. To conclude this section, I will pose the question, "Has King's 'dream' been realized, not merely recognized, by people across time?"

The middle section of this essay will include my personal recognition and realization of the fact of racism, which continues to be a cause of conflict and inequity for too many people, whether many people choose to acknowledge this reality or not. I will discuss when I first became aware of the issue of race, which was while I was riding the bus to school in kindergarten and listening to conversations of other children, who often repeat what they hear in their homes. I will also discuss my fear and anger when I learned about the ongoing existence of the Ku Klux Klan, which I would have assumed could have, or should have, been embarrassed into nothingness decades ago. This section will continue with thoughts and reflections I have based on what I have read, seen, heard, learned, and come to understand through academic study, personal experience, and contemplative prayer.

I will conclude this section of the essay with my opinion of the current situation of racism. For example, while many, perhaps most, people want to consider racism an issue of the past, too often we use words like "we" and "they" when referring to racial identity, which can only perpetuate divisive attitudes and be the source of ongoing conflict. In addition, there is so much anger that affects our inner feelings, and therefore our attitudes, habits, and interactions with those around us, as we interpret and respond to community and world events that resonate the sad reality of inequity and injustice.

The conclusion of this essay must be very powerful. It will begin by reiterating that Martin Luther King Jr. had a dream, and although most of us recognize the importance of this dream, the reality of it remains shrouded by ongoing and often hidden, or even unintended, attitudes and words and actions of prejudice. My conclusion will be that King's dream has not been realized, just recognized, and while recognition is an essential step toward resolution, it is not enough to make his dream a reality. Our understanding and efforts toward the elimination of racism must be more than a study in black and white. Rather, we must examine all areas of gray.

Our world is multicolored, multihued, and multi-issued. It is not acceptable to enable or perpetuate "we" and "they" attitudes, habits, and interactions that become the essence of our reality. We must build bridges. We must dab our collective fingers into the waters of change. We must begin the ripples of realization from recognition, and not let the waves fade. We must keep dabbing, creating waves of change that will take dreams of equity into ongoing realities of justice and peace. To realize King's dream, we cannot merely be satisfied with improvement. We must be committed to ongoing change, based in accurate understanding of the past, sensitive awareness of the present, and prudent wisdom for the unfolding needs of the future.

We can never truly resolve an issue, like racism, if an aspect of it is minimized, ignored, or overlooked. Instead, we must bravely join together in our exploration, understanding, and elimination of racism, without anger, without pride, without aggression, and without embellishment. There is motivation enough in the facts. We can make King's dream a reality, if we are united in hope, in humility, in assertiveness, and in accuracy. It is "us" that stops "us" from putting an end to racism, and honoring and realizing the work and dream of Martin Luther King Jr. And so, let it be "us" that furthers "us" in fairness, in justice, in equality, which is true peace. We, the people of all races, are the roots of future humanity, recognizing the need for change, and bringing about the reality of the future, filled with dreams come true.

I have a dream that one day, we will all come together as a family in the human race for equality. I have a dream that one day, we will truly throw down our weapons, and love our differences. We will not fight, but neither will we erase history, or be blindly ignorant to that which has already unfolded. We will not be afraid, nor will we be angry, nor will we hate, nor will we be the cause of any suffering. We will be united in hope. I have a dream that we shall overcome, so that one day we can truly hold hands as one family, with all the colors of God's rainbow of life unfolding like a majestic tapestry, woven with threads of justice. I have a dream that one day we shall recognize and realize a "just peace," and proclaim in one voice to all of the earth, "Free at last, free at last, thank God almighty, King's dream has come true, and we *are* free at last!"

Recipe for Peace

Peace is possible.
Make peace an attitude.
Want it.
Make peace a habit.
Live it.
Make peace a reality.
Share it.
Peace is possible.
Make peace matter.
Our matter.
Make peace a priority.
Our priority.
Make peace a choice.
Our choice.
Peace is possible.

We must
Think gently,
Speak gently,
Live gently.
Peace is possible.
Be happy with who you are.
Be happy with who others are.
Be happy that we Are.
Peace is possible.
Role model acceptance.
Love others.
Role model forgiveness.
Encourage others.
Role model tolerance.
Treasure others.
Peace is possible.
Peace is possible.
Peace is possible.

By Mattie J.T. Stepanek, May 12, 2002,
in *Reflections of a Peacemaker:
A Portrait Through Heartsongs*
(Andrews McMeel Publishing, 2005)

PEACE IS POSSIBLE

Living to be 101 years old was one of the many goals I set for myself as a very young child. In the naive thinking of a four-year-old, I was not completely aware of the challenge it would be for anyone to live such a long life. But even as a little boy, I knew that living 101 years would be a great personal challenge for me, because I was born with a frightening disease that causes my body to die a little more and a little more each year, even during my infancy and youth. Many people, especially medical professionals, have been pleasantly surprised, and grateful, that I have lived to become a teenager. Now, at thirteen and a half years of age, even I am relieved, and thrilled, to have earned the respectful ranking of having so many years in my mortal moments.

But lately, I have found myself reflecting on my longtime goal of old age, and reconsidering what motivated me to desire such an extended presence here. I love living. I love people. I love nature. I love the earth. I love being able to wake up each day to the opportunities of yet another sunrise, knowing that I am alive, again. I love being able to inhale, and exhale with the words "thank you" whispered in the spirit of my breath as I make it into each next moment. I love the symbolic fading of every sunset, as the reality of each passing day settles gloriously or gently or even shadowed into the whatever that comes with lunar reflection, as we cycle into our next tomorrow. I love believing that I am making some difference in life that helps someone, somewhere, think or speak or live just a little more gently, a little more hopeful, a little more peaceful. So why am I now concerned, even hesitant, about the goal of living so many more decades?

It is not the reality and progression of my disease that scares me. Although my body is in great physical pain at times, I can handle whatever it is that I need to go through to keep my spirit present on earth mingled with my mortality awhile longer. I am not looking forward to being dead, because I love being alive, and I love being able to talk with and be with and play with and even hug and hold hands with my mom and my friends. And I have to admit that while I am afraid of "dying"—of the actual physical pain and struggle to breathe and the unknowns surrounding the event that transpires—I am not afraid of death. I am confident that there is something bigger and better than anything we can imagine in the here and now that awaits the goodness of our eternal spirit after the frailty of our ephemeral body dies.

What scares me most right now about living to be 101 years old is the sad threat of violence and war, and the real existence of inequity and injustice. I know that conflict has apparently always existed. And I know that conflict has led to violence throughout recorded history. But it also seems that as time passes, we are growing too accustomed to war and injustice. I imagine a world many years ago, where violence was unfortunately real, but reports of murders or bombings or other horrors were shocking. I am aware that life is not that simple, and that even in history, too many people have turned a blind eye toward poverty and a curious eye toward a public execution. But it seems that there is so much violence and poverty and injustice in the world nowadays that it cannot all be reported. And even when it is reported, our minds and spirits are not always touched or moved to become involved in changing attitudes and habits and realities that shape the world, and the future.

More and more in recent years, the papers and programs delivering the latest news only mention the most horrific of events, or situations that are either unusual or serial in nature. Today, even children affected by inequity and violence are only newsworthy if they are extraordinarily young, or if a large group of young people are affected simultaneously. It is as if we have become insensitive to many issues and realities that hurt individuals and groups of people in our own communities and around the world. I believe that people are genuinely and generally good, but I am witnessing a lack of respect by so many people, and for so many people.

There is a growing lack of respect by people for themselves, for others, for nature, for life, for the needs of so many in the world. Concurrently, there is a growing sense of self-justification in acts of violence, of righteousness in acts of retaliation, of desperateness in acts of preservation, and of rectitude in acts of liberation by force. For me as a young teenager, as a member of a family and a community, as a citizen of the world, it is frightening and dismaying, even horrifying.

There are so many weapons being created and stored and readied around the world, that we risk mass destruction and slow decay with every passing day, and every exchanged blow and word. Conflict is inevitable. But the needs and fear that lead to hate and suffering are unnecessary. No child or adult should have to fall asleep fearing the blast of a sniper's bullet, or the silent release of chemicals or germs into the air we must breathe.

Courage is being brave when there is something to fear. Right now, we need to be committed to the strength of courage. As we move forward in a world filled with the fears of unknowns and differences and war and poverty, we need to be brave in our commitment to planning peace. We need to be determined that there are things worth fighting for, like human needs and civil rights, and that we can effectively battle without violence. Doing so, however, will take creativity and perseverance and fortitude, as we serve as advocates and activists and role models in the name of justice and peace.

INTERGENERATIONAL CAREGIVING

Not long ago, I was invited to prepare and deliver the opening remarks for a conference being organized and sponsored by the Rosalynn Carter Institute. When Mrs. Carter called and asked me to work with her on this event I was honored and excited, knowing that it would be a wonderful opportunity to participate in a project headed by someone like her. Mrs. Carter and her husband, Jimmy, are genuinely caring individuals who work very hard for people, for the world, and for many different aspects of peace. But after I spoke with her I began to wonder what meaningful and useful thoughts I, as a young teenager, would be able to offer the adults in attendance, all of whom were already experts on the issue being addressed.

The topic being explored was "intergenerational caregiving," a concept that in name alone represents both an important and an essential effort. I decided to begin with a poem I had written, called "Flowing Thoughtfulness," which could serve to set the tone for understanding that even small acts of kindness can have a great effect on others, and then look carefully at what the words—inter, generational, care, and giving—really mean.

I found that "inter" is defined in dictionaries as a prefix meaning between or among. It is also defined as reciprocal, which implies equality, and give and take. According to dictionaries, the root word "generational" comes from "generate," which means to produce or to create. I reasoned, therefore, that while the word "generation" typically refers to a particular age group such as youth, adults, or the elderly, that it also means production and creation.

"Care" was an easy word to consider. Even without a dictionary it is known that to care is to be concerned about something, to take notice, or to nurture. But dictionaries detail that the word "care" also means to take caution, to be watchful or vigilant, to provide protection, guardianship or safekeeping, and even to worry. "Giving" was another easy word to think about. To be giving is defined as being generous, benevolent, charitable, and even open-handed.

A wonderful list of words had been collected as I merely examined the title and focus of the conference. Openhanded safekeeping. Watchful nurturing. Concerned protection. And all of this from an intergenerational group of people, not limited by age, or race, or gender, or nationality, or religion, or ability, or any other boundary. Yes, a group of people who produce solutions and create the future in a gentle, compassionate way.

Oftentimes, people use the idea of concentric circles to illustrate a point. This is especially true when considering ideas in which one or more people or events are supported or affected by the existence or actions of one or more other people or events. At the center of the circle might be a child, then a parent in the next protective ring, and a grandparent in the outermost ring. Well, any individual could be at the center of the circle, at any given time. It could be an infant born with a severe disability, or a young adult after a car accident, or a middle-aged person who has had a stroke, or someone in their seventies with Alzheimer's disease. It could also be a starving child who was born into poverty, or a teenager handed a rifle in a war-torn area, or an adult dying from a treatable disease, or an elderly individual jailed under discriminatory laws.

At the center of the circle could even be an individual of any age who is caring for any of the individuals in the examples. It could be a family member. It could be someone who is not yet born. It could be me. It could be any of the people I would be addressing. It could be anybody who reads these words at any point in time. The point is, I realized that if we really consider what "intergenerational caregiving" means, then we will know that we need to start the concentric circles of support and care rippling. We need to collectively dab our fingers, of all ages, into the waters, and spread the idea of intergenerational caregiving around the room, around the community, around the country, and around the world.

I knew that rippling this idea of "flowing thoughtfulness" around the room would be the easy part, because those in attendance would have already made a decision, a commitment, to the task of studying, strengthening, and spreading the principles and programs of exemplary intergenerational caregiving. And I knew that intergenerational caregiving was a key component of supporting aspects of peace for individuals, and for the world. It was my hope, though, that those gathered at the conference would be motivated to continue with the more difficult task of taking these ideas out to others, of spreading peace in additional circles. Change begins with the attitudes and habits and realities lived by each individual. It continues to grow as we help others understand what peace means, and why peace matters, and how to become involved with family and neighbors and others around the world. We all could make a peaceful difference for those who need to be at the center of a circle of gentle care, supported by the ripples of intergenerational caregiving.

HOPEFUL LIVING

As I consider my concerns and fears about the ongoing reality of war and inequity, I must recommit myself to believing in the possibility of a just peace, of intergenerational caregiving, and in my own message of hope. I must remain determined, and confident, that people and organizations seeking and planning peace will make a difference, not only in achieving specific steps toward peace, but also in raising awareness and sensitivity to the needs and experiences of so many people in the world. I must remember to have courage to live whatever undetermined length of time I have on earth, making each day something that matters for the future.

I believe that justice can prevail. But I also believe that a just peace relies on individuals and organizations uniting in a common goal. With careful planning, through lessons learned from the successes and failures of those before us, just peace can be a reality for each of us each day.

We cannot change the history of the past. The past can never be altered, merely observed. But we can learn lessons from that which has already occurred, and from people who were, and are, able and willing to share their thoughts, their insights, their experiences. We can study what events and approaches have made a positive or powerful impact, and we can realize what events and approaches should never be allowed to happen again. The past is a valuable tool for planning peace and for securing justice in our world.

We cannot know the mystery of the future. The future can never be calculated, merely speculated. But we can prepare for a just cause that will last for all ages.

We cannot ignore our gift of the present. The present can always be an opportunity to act, to balance observation and speculation, to make a difference. It is the aspect of time that can be touched, affected. The present is the space where the past and future meet, where they join. The present is where what was unfolds into what will be. The present is each moment. And the present is where a just peace is possible.

In the Old Testament of the Bible, a man known as Moses calls out to his creator, his supreme being, his God, and asks "by what name shall I call you?" The translation of the response to Moses was profound in simplicity— "I AM." Think about it. I AM. Not "I was." Not "I will be." Not "I would if I could." Not "I might if someone else does something first." Not even "I should." Simply, "I AM." And that is simply how I choose to see the great and profound mosaic of life—filled with complexities and uniqueness and differences, and the past touching the future exactly when and where and how it unfolds in the present of each moment. A just peace is profound in its simplicity. I am. We are. Life is.

Mattie and his friends Kyle and Travis Bouchard playfully demonstrating an approach to being peaceful, July 2002.

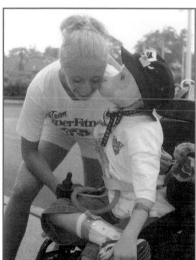

Mattie having fun just being a kid and enjoying a day at the Cincinnati Zoo with Tara and other members of the Hemelgarn family, May 2002.

I AM

I am black.
I am white.
I am all skins in between.
I am young.
I am old.
I am each age that has been.
I am scrawny.
I am well fed.
I am starving for attention.
I am famous.
I am cryptic.
I am hardly worth the mention.
I am short.
I am height.
I am any frame or stature.
I am smart.
I am challenged.
I am striving for a future.

I am able.
I am weak.
I am some strength, I am none.
I am being.
I am thought.
I am all things said and done.
I am born.
I am died.
I am dust of humble roots.
I am grace.
I am pain.
I am labor of willed fruits.
I am a slave.
I am free.
I am bonded to my life.
I am rich.
I am poor.
I am wealth amid strife.

I am shadow.

I am glory.

I am hiding from my shame.

I am hero.

I am loser.

I am yearning for a name.

I am empty.

I am proud.

I am seeking my tomorrow.

I am growing.

I am fading.

I am hope amid the sorrow.

I am certain.

I am doubtful.

I am desperate for solutions.

I am leader.

I am student.

I am faith and evolutions.

I am spirit.

I am voice.

I am memory not recalled.

I am chance.

I am cause.

I am effort, blocked and walled.

I am hymn.

I am heard.

I am reason without rhyme.

I am past.

I am nearing.

I am present in all times.

I am many.

I am no one.

I am seasoned by each being.

I am me.

I am you.

I am all souls now decreeing . . .

I AM.

By Mattie J.T. Stepanek, February 4, 2001,
in *Celebrate Through Heartsongs*
(Hyperion/VSP, 2002)

E-mail from: Jimmy Carter
Date: December 16, 2003 6:06 AM EST
To: Mattie J.T. Stepanek
Subject: Greetings

Mattie: I've heard about your Christmas activities, and the joy you give to little Kaylee. Best wishes with your book signings. I've been promoting my new novel for about three weeks, finishing this past Friday. It's been a good success, moving up now to number six on the *New York Times* list. I've found that there is a lot more competition in the fiction field than non-fiction, with Harry Potter, Stephen King, *The Da Vinci Code,* and the prolific murder mystery writers. It took me seven years to write the book, with all the research I had to do to make the Revolutionary War accounts as accurate as possible and to bring the fictional characters to life.

I had to take off a few days to go to Geneva, where the new proposal for Middle East peace was announced. Despite its condemnation from extremists from both sides, I think it offers an unavoidable pattern if peace is ever to come to the region.

Rosalynn and I leave this afternoon for Bolivia, the little landlocked nation in South America. The country is coming apart politically, and we'll be trying to reconcile some of the warring political parties. The recently elected president (a friend of ours) was forced into exile in October, and is now living in Washington. One of the big squabbles is how much coca can be grown legally. As you may know, the native Indians have chewed the leaves for centuries, but some of it is processed into cocaine and exported illegally to the United States. The natives comprise about two-thirds of the total population, and have been excluded from their fair role in the government. It's a complicated situation, which we hope to understand better after this trip. We'll return next Sunday, and will be home for Christmas, with most of our children and grandchildren. You may wish to look up La Paz, the capital, on the Internet. It's the highest capital in the world.

We'll have to miss the first showings of the new *Lord of the Rings* movie, but will see it next week. I hope you'll have a chance to enjoy it. All of us Carters send you our best wishes. Your friendship is one of my most cherished possessions.

You have my love, and prayers. Jimmy Carter

Mattie loved being an "uncle" to his "neighbor niece," Kaylee Dobbins, the granddaughter of Sandy Newcomb (his "very favorite adult best friend"). After spending four months in the intensive care unit, Mattie was happy to be home and able to hold Kaylee for hours at a time during June 2003.

E-mail from: Mattie J.T. Stepanek
Date: December 16, 2003 12:48 PM EST
To: Jimmy Carter
Subject: (no subject)

Dear Jimmy,

Thank you so much for your e-mail. I love hearing from you. And I was so proud of you on Larry King. You did great. You are so honest and you inspire me. I was sorry that I couldn't come to say hello in person since you were within an hour of where I live. But my trachea and fingers are bleeding again, and my autonomic system is trying to fail (notice I said "trying" because I am not going to let it happen). I do have to go to the hospital a lot more since I decided that I don't want to be in the ICU this time. You can't "live" in the ICU . . . you just exist. And I want to do the "Just Peace" book with you. Which is why I am writing. I [will be sending you another e-mail and] attaching a file (it has no virus so it is safe) that has a possible outline for the book and a list of possible people to be interviewed [and the possible questions]. The people interviewed would comment on the questions posed throughout my outline of sections to be included. I am open to any feedback you have about the outline, the questions, and the people I want to interview. I am sorry it has taken me so long to do the research on the people, but my mom made me take the summer off, and my health began to change again during late October. I got scared for a while. Now I'm just stubborn and am getting back to work. I am truly committed to the project. I am looking forward to hearing from you. And please tell Rosalynn that I send my love. The best part of my summer, other than MDA Summer Camp, was speaking with and for her. What an honor.

I love you very much, Mattie

Oh, PS: Thank you very much for the copy of your new book. And CONGRATULATIONS on making the *New York Times* best-seller list for fiction!!! I am so proud of you and all your hard work.

Mattie (third from left) poses with Virginia Wheeler; Laura, Annie, and Diane Tresca; and Flora and Paul Beaudet (L to R) at the Buddha's Art of Healing exhibit in Washington, D.C., summer 1998. Every day for a week, Mattie watched the monks create a colorful sand "healing mendala." (Above) Mattie poses with one of the monks during the closing ceremonies.

Buddhist monks create the mendala.

E-mail from: Mattie J.T. Stepanek
Date: December 16, 2003 1:35 PM EST
To: Jimmy Carter
Subject: Just Peace book interviews

Dear Jimmy,

I have been giving a lot of thought to the interviews for our book, "Just Peace," and to the essential questions that I would ask each of the people who will be involved. It is very exciting to think that I will have the opportunity to learn from individuals who have worked so hard to bring peace to so many people, and at so many different levels. And it will be an honor to work with you on integrating their responses—their memories, their experiences, their opinions, their ideas, their understanding, and their hopes—into a practical plan for peace.

As a person who spends a lot of time reading and then journaling my personal reflections from the facts and insights I have gathered, considering who I would have a "meeting of the minds" with is a fascinating process. But it is also one that is requiring a lot of thought and ongoing research. What's interesting is that even before we discussed this book, I have often wondered who I would choose to spend time with if I were granted the opportunity of fifteen minutes with any three individuals in the world from the past, from the present, and from the future. Imagine the lessons of and for humanity we could learn.

The future is an easy consideration, because there are no names or knowns to sift through, and I would simply choose the people who represented three things that matter very much to me right now. I would choose to learn from whoever truly brings about a just peace at all levels for all people in all nations, I would choose to talk with whoever discovers the cure to neuromuscular and other diseases that take the lives of children, and I would choose to be with my grandchildren.

As a peacemaker, I know that I would carefully choose for my opportunity to meet with three people from the past. There are activists I could learn from who, like Martin Luther King Jr., have been awarded the Nobel Peace Prize for their efforts, such as Jane Addams, a great mediator who was recognized in 1931 for her role in changing the lives of many women and children, and Ralph Bunche, who in 1950 was the first black person to receive the award, for his work on the Palestine Commission through the United Nations. Mother Teresa, the leader of the Order of the Missionaries of Charity in India, was recognized by the Nobel committee in 1979 for her untiring commitment and service to the poor. I would want to ask Mother Teresa, not just why, but how she was able to selflessly reach out and care for all people, regardless of their health or wealth or condition or contribution, expecting absolutely nothing in return.

There are also historical activists who fought nonviolently for peace and equity, like Mahatma Gandhi, who have not been awarded a grand prize for their efforts.

But the lessons I could learn from humanitarians like Eleanor Roosevelt, Margaret Meade, and Princess Diana are just as valuable as the lessons from individuals who have been officially recognized for their work. I can only imagine the powerful inspiration and practical information I could gather from people like these three, who advocated for the needs and rights and education of citizens from their own and other countries.

The most difficult decision, and one that I am now considering as I plan to invite people to work with me on this book, is who I should choose from the present world that could teach us more about the "why" and "how" of planning all different aspects of peace. There are so many commendable individuals seeking peace in so many different ways and who are making such a difference for our world.

To organize my thoughts and efforts, I have decided to group role models I have studied into categories such as political or spiritual leaders striving for peace, or celebrities using the power of their name to advocate for humanitarian efforts, or the everyday "ordinary" people of the world who do whatever they can to make a positive difference in a nonviolent but powerful way. And in choosing who to learn from, I will also consider the various types of peace we need in our world, such as attaining inner peace, meeting the basic needs of all people, seeking equity in human and civil rights, developing and maintaining peaceful relationships within and between families and groups and countries, and achieving a balance of respect and peace between people and nature and the earth on which we all live.

There are two attachments to this note. The first is a draft listing individuals that I think have valuable lessons to offer. I have included a bit of information about some of the people. But this is an ongoing effort and I am still making notes about many of the people I have studied. So, some of the people have information listed, but others just have a name and identifying comment, because I have read enough to know that they have made a difference and can teach us lessons but have not made formal notes yet.

The second attachment is my thoughts on the types of questions I would like to ask the people who choose to be interviewed. I think they are essential questions that we should all be asking ourselves in life. Please let me know what you think about the list, and who you would suggest I study more about, and who you think may be willing to work with me and be interviewed for this book. And please let me know what you think about the questions, too.

I am very excited to be working on this book with you. We are peacemakers from different generations, but with common hopes. I have learned so much from you. I am trying to make a peaceful difference in the world, like you and with you, for everyone. Please tell your wife and family that I said hello, and that I think of them often. I love hearing the stories you share about them in your letters to me, and in your books.

Love, Mattie

First Attachment to December 16, 2003, E-mail

Political leaders

- Jimmy Carter (Nobel Peace Prize 2002; mediation; world harmony through political efforts; promoting international economic and social development)
- John Hume and David Trimble (Nobel Peace Prize 1998; efforts to find a peaceful solution to the conflict in Northern Ireland)
- Kofi Annan (Nobel Peace Prize 2001; United Nations Secretary General)
- Aung San Suu Kyi (Nobel Peace Prize 1991; a peaceful oppositional leader; human rights advocate from Burma; currently on "house arrest")
- General Colin Powell (U.S. Secretary of State; U.S. military leader)
- Queen Noor Al Hussein (former queen of Jordan; work in trying to rid the world of weapons)
- Queen Rania (current queen of Jordan; strong voice advocating for the human rights of all people, especially those caught in the ongoing crises in the Middle East; appeals for improving application of humanitarian laws; " . . . against any aggression committed against any innocent civilians, irrespective of the perpetrator or the victim. We do not approve of any aggression . . ."; violent assaults intended to "dismantle the infrastructure of terrorism" often result in "dismantling the infrastructure for peace.")

Spiritual leaders

- Tenzin Gyatso (Nobel Peace Prize 1989; fourteenth Dalai Lama of Tibet; left home country rather than fight; prayerful, nonviolent protest)
- Archbishop Desmond Tutu (Nobel Peace Prize 1984; former secretary general of the South African Council of Churches; nonviolent efforts against apartheid; improvement of human and civil rights; teaches people to remember hardships of the past as lessons for the future; cherish all aspects of life)
- Pope John Paul II (leader of the Roman Catholic Church; written many books about peace, reconciliation)
- Thich Nhat Hanh (writer/speaker; gaining peace through love; honoring all aspects of life; forgiveness)

Civil and human rights advocates

- Nelson Mandela (Nobel Peace Prize 1993; spent twenty-seven years in South African prison because of racial injustice; nonviolent advocate to end apartheid; improve civil and human rights; became president of South Africa)
- Marian Wright Edelman (strong advocate for justice; needs and rights of children; basic security; education)
- Coretta Scott King (daughter of Martin Luther King Jr.; continuing King's work; activist; tolerance)

- Lech Walesa (Nobel Peace Prize 1983; Polish Solidarity; human rights; nonviolent protest)
- Reverend Jesse Jackson (civil rights activist; prayerful courage; speeches; travel; mediation)

Humanitarians (celebrities)

- Oprah Winfrey (movie/television celebrity; generosity; compassion; Angel Network of South Africa; power of celebrity status to set example for others to share resources, time, energy, money; prayerful; provisions for education; human needs/rights; perseverance during personal adversity)
- Jerry Lewis (movie/television celebrity; advocacy; commitment; National Spokesperson for Muscular Dystrophy Association; power of celebrity status to make a difference in lives of people with life-threatening conditions; perseverance even when criticized)
- Larry King (television celebrity; power of interview/talk show to inform/educate others about issues of peace, civil/human rights, catastrophic needs; current events; honesty; straightforward)

Humanitarians (artists)

- Maya Angelou (poet; professional skill for remembering history and improving future; civil/human rights)
- Elie Wiesel (Holocaust survivor; writer; philosopher; lessons from horror; keeping faith in people and God; peaceful resolution; letting go of grudges)
- Nile Rodgers (award-winning music artist who founded the We Are Family Foundation in response to terrorist acts to promote global tolerance, education, respect, and peace)
- Steven Spielberg (movie director/writer; creative portrayal of historic events to remind people of the horrors of war, evil of violence; professional skill for peaceful endeavors through creativity/entertainment)

Nature and Earth advocates

- Jane Goodall (research; animal/environmental protection; peace with the earth; education)
- Art Shegonee (Native American, Menominee/Potowatomi tribe; member of Call for Peace Drum & Dance Company; respect for earth, life, nature; educational programs for children)
- Jean-Michel Cousteau (son of Jacques Cousteau; research; education; protect and respect earth and sea)

Ordinary citizens

- Ron Wyatt (Washington, D.C., police officer; worked for United Nations in Kosovo

for one year as international police monitor; shared professional skills to help secure human/civil rights in war-torn country)
- Kelly Ellison (Executive Director of the Children's Peace Pavilion; key effort in the development of "Peace Educators" and "PaxCorps" programs)
- Paula Beckman (Early Childhood Special Education; University of Maryland; founded International Partners; travels regularly to El Salvador to bring educational/medical supplies to children/families in war-torn/poor regions)
- Children from war-torn and poverty stricken-regions (e.g., Palestine, Israel, Iraq, Afganistan, U.S. Appalachian region)

Second Attachment to December 16, 2003, E-mail

List of possible questions, "Just Peace" book interviews:
In one sentence, what would you like people to know about you today?
Why do you think conflict and violence exist?
Do you think that war has been necessary in the past?
Do you think that conflict and war have changed across history?
Do you think that war is ever justified?
Why do we wage war in some situations, and avoid it in other similar situations?
How do you think that conflicts should be settled?
How have you been involved in peacekeeping efforts?
What are the greatest challenges to peacekeeping efforts?
What do you consider your greatest contribution toward peace?
Do you think that world peace could, or
    will, ever be a reality?
What message of peace would you give to
    children and adults today?
What is your philosophy for life?
How do you want the world to
    remember you?
Is there anything else you would
    like to add?

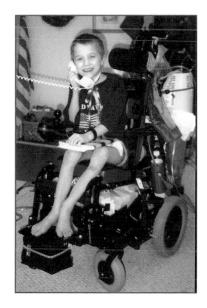

Mattie enjoyed many phone conversations with his "real-life heroes," including Jimmy Carter, Oprah Winfrey, and Jerry Lewis. Their topics ranged from prayer and peacemaking to playing baseball and practical jokes.

E-mail from: Jimmy Carter
Date: December 16, 2003 4:05 PM EST
To: Mattie J.T. Stepanek
Subject: Thanks

To Mattie: I just received your message and am leaving for Bolivia in a few minutes. Hurriedly: I like the outline, will do the foreword and be interviewed, and like the list of others. With two exceptions, I know them all. It will be much better if you ask them personally, perhaps by sending them some preprepared questions. I'm sure they will be eager to respond. I'll help in any way you ask.

Love, Jimmy

Mattie shares his message of Heartsongs with Oprah Winfrey during his first appearance on her show in October 2001. Mattie and Oprah developed a close friendship, e-mailing and phoning each other on a regular basis. Through the years, Mattie became a frequent and favorite guest on Oprah's show. During Mattie's funeral celebration, Oprah shared a powerful tribute honoring Mattie, based on their conversations and Internet interactions.

E-mail from: Kelly Ellison, Executive Director, Children's Peace Pavilion
Date: December 27, 2003
To: Mattie Stepanek
Subject: "Peace Is Possible" exhibit

Dear Mattie:

Thanks so much for visiting with me about our new exhibit in the Children's Peace Pavilion that will focus on your message of peace and hope. We had fun working out the details of the exhibit with you. Soon, kids from all over the world can visit the CPP museum and learn about how "peace really is possible!" We are planning a special area for kids to create their own poems and artwork. We know your Heartsong books and artwork will be an inspiration to thousands of children who wish to make a difference in this world. We plan to open the exhibit in April of 2004 in conjunction with our annual conference that will be attended by several hundred children from around the world. We hope you'll be able to join us and "cut the ribbon" on your "Peace Is Possible" exhibit.

Below this letter you will find some of the information you asked about to use in your upcoming speeches about peace. It explains a bit about our mission and projects. I have also added some excerpts from an article that was written after you delivered your speech here last year! Give our best to your mom, Jeni, and to Micah the "peace puppy"!

Love, Kelly and the Children's Peace Pavilion Team

Attached Information About CPP

- The mission of the Children's Peace Pavilion is to *enrich the lives of children through the pursuit of peace for all.* This is a unique, interactive children's museum focusing on teaching the essential elements of peace. The "Pavilion," which means shelter, offers children and families opportunities to explore, experiment, and learn the concept of peace in a fun, safe, hands-on environment. The museum houses more than twenty-five exhibits that teach life skills such as self-appreciation, self-confidence, emotional literacy, communication, cooperation, conflict resolution, diversity, and stewardship. Each year thousands of children are engaged in events and activities that focus around the universal message of peace. The purpose of the Children's Peace Pavilion exhibits and programs are to empower children and adults with the peacemaking skills they need to make responsible choices. Once participants learn these basic life skills they can make choices that create a future without fear; a future of hope and peace.

• A Children's Peace Pavilion exhibit centered around Mattie J.T. Stepanek's "Peace Is Possible" message will be unveiled in April 2004. In addition to learning about this young peacemaker and his Heartsongs poetry, children can enjoy creating their own poetry with magnetized words, finger painting their visualization of peace, and discussing Mattie's "Three Choices for Peace." Mattie's mission will continue to inspire the museum's visitors and staff for years to come.

• Peace Champions is a membership program of the Children's Peace Pavilion. The objective of Peace Champions is to reach children of all ages with the possibilities of peace. We accomplish this by providing children, young adults, parents, and families with the resources they need to connect to the museum's concepts and programs and learn the skills of peacemaking. Anyone can join Peace Champions and start the process of making peace possible!

• Certified Peace Educators (CPE) is a graduate-level certificate program being developed in partnership with Graceland University to recognize formal and informal educators and community leaders who wish to attain a certain level of proficiency in the field of peace education at regional and national levels. A distance and residential education program will launch in August 2006.

• Excerpts from "'Everybody has a Heartsong'—poet and peacemaker Mattie Stepanek," *Herald* Vol. 149 No. 7, July 2002, Community of Christ, pp 25-26: "Mattie is our mission in action," said Children's Peace Pavilion Executive Director Kelly Ellison. "There's a synergy between what we do and what Mattie does," she said. Mattie's message mirrors our mission and introduces adults and children to the Peace Pavilion's comprehensive peace education programs focusing on the four concepts of peace: Peace for Me, Peace for Us, Peace for Everyone, and Peace for the Planet. "We really accomplished our goal," Kelly said, "furthering the mission of the Pavilion with Mattie's visit addressing more than 5,000 children with his message of peace and hope. This was more than a one-time event. We hope a long-term relationship has been built between Mattie and the Pavilion based on our shared philosophy for peace."

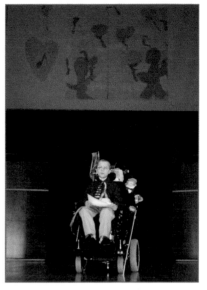

Mattie pointing to the Peace Assembly sign announcing his keynote address, May 2002.

Mattie delivering his first "peace speech" to more than 5,000 children at the Children's Peace Pavilion in Independence, Missouri, May 2002.

Mattie shows off CPP staff member Jeremy Kohlman's bald head, shaved for his role as Gandhi during their performance during the Peace Assembly, May 2002.

Mattie and his mom work together playing "Humano Harambe" at the Children's Peace Pavilion museum, May 2002.

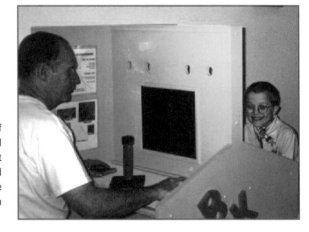

Mattie and CPP staff member Sandy Twitchell enjoy a block game that encourages listening and communication at the Children's Peace Pavilion museum, May 2002.

Mattie playing in the "Harmony Hopping" music and lights section of the museum with his mom, Jeni.

Mattie putting on a puppet show in the Children's Peace Pavilion museum.

Mattie listens to Lauren Lindsey read her winning entry in the CPP poetry contest as Executive Director Kelly Ellison looks on.

Taking a break to play "limbo" with some of the other participants in the 2002 Peace Assembly in Independence, Missouri.

In April 2004, the Children's Peace Pavilion in Independence, Missouri, unveiled the "Mattie J.T. Stepanek: Peace Is Possible" exhibit. CPP Executive Director Kelly Ellison worked with Mattie to design the two rooms of hands-on activities that encourage children to consider and share feelings through poetry and finger painting.

Sandy Newcomb reads the messages on the "Three Choices for Peace" display.

Mattie's dog, "peace puppy" Micah, relaxes near part of his "daddy's" exhibit, May 2005.

Final Thoughts

Have you ever wondered
If some people will cry, and cry
And sigh after you die?
Have you wondered
If the people will cry and then
Try to move forward as time
Fades the wounds and
Dries the tears and
Gracefully blesses the soul?
I have.
I have so
Wondered.
Have you ever wondered
If some people will live, and live
And love differently after you pass?
Have you wondered
If the people will live and then
Sift and reflect on the
Wisdom of your thoughts and the
Gentleness of your words and the
Enduring consequences of your actions?
I have.
I have so, so
Wondered.
Have you ever wondered
If some people will wonder, and wonder
And wander in realization after reality rests?
Have you wondered
If the people will wonder and then
Peacefully ponder the undying
Essence of your echo and the epitaphic
Silhouette of your legacy that
Spirits the memory after death arises?
I have.
I have so, so, so
Wondered.

By Mattie J.T. Stepanek, March 7, 2004,
in *Reflections of a Peacemaker: A Portrait Through Heartsongs*
(Andrews McMeel Publishing, 2005)

JUST PEACE: AN ENDEAVOR

When we envision world peace, we imagine something that feels good. We think about harmony, and tranquility, and serenity. In a peaceful world, there is no fighting. There is no war. There is no arguing, no greed, no meanness, no hate. Fear and guilt are not a part of peaceful resolutions, because with peace there are no ulterior motives hidden in minds or hearts. There is a gentle quietness to peace. Relinquishing anger and tight-fistedness brings a calming acceptance and resilience. Peace is something that feels good when we recognize and realize it inside of us. And, we can feel the goodness of peace when we are selfless and reconciled with others, and when we are considerate and careful with the earth.

Conflict will inevitably be a part of personal and societal life. However, peace is possible, even though planning for and achieving world peace is an elaborate, complex, and vast endeavor. Accepting, believing in, and committing to such a venture requires unbiased deliberation, open-mind-edness, reflection, and steadfast allegiance to balancing the needs and rights of all people in an equitable, unified, and nonviolent manner.

Courage and creativity are essential to seeking and planning peace. So, too, are other altruistic qualities, such as honesty, humility, and integrity, as representatives from many nations, faiths, and economic situations come together to consider and launch accords that will secure civil liberties and provide for the basic needs of all people. The development of true peace and justice also obliges some level of sacrifice as we balance the varied needs and rights of so many people and cultures and environmental states. The concept of sacrifice in seeking peace need not be considered something negative, like a cost or a surrender. Rather, sacrifice is a positive paradigm of yielding, of accepting, of recognizing and realizing that the needs and rights of one person or group should not, and must not, be gained at the cost of ignoring or infringing on the needs and rights of another person or group.

There are people who will claim that war is sometimes the only path to peace, and that sometimes, only invading and conquering through acts of violence will result in change. The impact of war results in change, but it is change by force, which is very different than the careful creation of something equitable. War is not just. And the risk of war can no longer be justified, even when there is a clear need for change that will secure human and civil rights. It is never right to kill, but in the present, with weapons of mass destruction and mayhem instead of rules for war, it is also too perilous.

A great speaker once said, "We have slain the dragon of evil that we have been fighting all these years. But alas, out of the ashes are born thousands of evil, poisonous snakes." We cannot conquer hatred and inequity with violence; that only begets more hatred and inequity. If we brave our fears, and learn about the needs and gifts of our neighbors with compassion and appreciation, we can and will defeat every last snake, and ensure a future filled with hope and peace. And if we pause for a moment and consider the task at hand, we may realize that planning peace can be profound in its simplicity.

Truly, peace is built through negotiation and mediation, which can be lengthy and sometimes even frustrating. But peace is worthy, and peace is just, and peace is necessary. Planning and waging peace is not only the safest risk for our future, it is also the only way our world and we, the people, can truly survive the technological advancements that threaten our existence. We must consider what will happen to us and to our future if we do not plan peace. If we do survive this particular war-torn period of time, what do we expect next, for ourselves and for our descendants?

THREE CHOICES FOR PEACE

My thoughts on planning peace are rooted in the concept of "choice." Everything in life has choice, even if the only choice we have is the attitude with which we embrace each moment. I believe that peace is possible because I believe a plan for peace is rooted in three simple choices we each can and must make, for ourselves and for our world.

First, we must choose to make peace an attitude. We must want it. We must make it something that really matters. Peace begins inside of each of us. We must be satisfied, happy, with who we are as a person, and we must accept that people are good, that life is good, even with the many inevitable conflicts and natural suffering that will exist. We must choose to see possibilities—tasks, chores, sharing, even donations of money, time, energy, and other resources—as opportunities to make a difference. In choosing to make peace an attitude, we are making it something that matters in every thought, in every situation, in every hope, for every person.

Second, we must choose to make peace a habit. We must live it. We cannot just think about peace and hope for peace. We must also choose to develop habits, ways of speaking and acting, that model peaceful attributes and that promote peaceful interactions. We need to choose to let go of petty differences and disagreements. We need to reconsider why we are arguing with our family members, with our neighbors, with other countries, and we need to remember how precious life really is. We need to make words and phrases like "thank you" and "please" and "I care" and "welcome" and "after you" and "you are forgiven" and "I'm sorry" and "you matter" and "I love you" everyday vernacular. We need to smile, and hug, and shake hands, and do acts of kindness every day that let people witness and appreciate how gentle and caring the world can be.

And third, we must choose to make peace a reality. We must share it. We must seek opportunities to learn about other people—people we know and people we will never meet but who are a part of the mosaic of life. We must plan and inspire peace around the world through the gentleness and kindness of our thoughts and our words and our actions. We must get involved with and learn from organizations and individuals that seek peace and equity, that support people who are in some type of need, and that promote nonviolent conflict resolution.

If we simply, but profoundly, choose to make peace an attitude and a habit and a reality, peace is possible. If we are committed to pensive, poetic, and philosophical ways of thinking, and if we build practical, prayerful, and purposeful ways of living, peaceful friendships can be nurtured between and among groups around the world. Then, as we respectfully learn about other individuals and nations through education and involvement, we can seek to balance and provide for the basic needs and secure the civil and human rights of all people in an equitable and just manner. And in doing so, we grow together in humanity, treasuring our differences and endeavoring to rebuild the mosaic of life.

PEACEFUL LIVING

I believe that life is a journey. Some journeys are long, and some are short. Some are painful, and some are pleasant, but most journeys offer a mix of burdens and blessings. Each journey involves many decisions, some that will impact one's own life, and some that may trickle down through generations or grow to touch billions of lives. And, we can learn from every step of the journey. We can learn from our own lessons and decisions, and from the voices and choices of others.

While we cannot choose the life we are born into, we can choose how we embrace the moments we are given. I have chosen to live as a poet—reflective, creative, and expressive. I have chosen to live as a peacemaker—thinking gently, speaking gently, living gently, so that the world is reminded gently of the blessings of humanity. I have chosen to live as a philosopher—appreciating that the gift of life is short, sweet, and sacred. I have chosen to always remember to play after every storm—celebrating life every day, in some way, so that I have strength to persevere in whatever inevitable challenge awaits my next moment.

ON BEING PENSIVE Sometimes we are not aware of how good or how bad a situation can be until we talk to people who have lived through something that we have never experienced, or until we study about people and events that have shaped the world as it is today. The lessons embedded in memories, whether they are our own personal recollections or the shared contribution of others, and whether they reference successful endeavors or well-intentioned but failed attempts, are invaluable. Memories are a gift of the past that we hold in the present to create what can be a great future. Memories allow us to sift through lessons of the past without reliving it, and in doing so, we can realize what things are good to repeat, and we can heed the warning of things that should never be allowed to happen again. In choosing to be pensive, we can patiently take the bouldering mistakes of the past, and the roadblocking challenges of the present, and build stairs that support our climb into a positive and peaceful future.

It is also wise to have role models, who inspire us to think and to strive for specific attributes or goals we admire. Some of my role models include: Jimmy Carter, a humble peacemaker; Oprah Winfrey, a generous humanitarian; Jerry Lewis, an unwavering advocate; and, my mom, Jeni Stepanek, a caring person who has given me life, and saved my life, and guided my life as I have journeyed through lessons in endurance, commitment, and strength of character. I have learned many lessons from my role models, and from people I have studied or read about across the years. And when I am faced with a difficult decision, whether it is a decision of attitude or of action, I pensively consider how my role models would respond or act.

While we can look up to people, even admire them and try to "be like" them, we should never try to "be" someone else. It is important for each of us to be satisfied with who we are as our own selves. We should try to be our best self, but not compare ourselves to others. Respecting others and the earth begins with self-respect, which is rooted in self-confidence and contentment. There is nothing wrong with seeking personal or professional achievements or prosperity, but we must also redefine our concepts of what it means to be "successful" and to make a "valuable contribution" to society. Pensive attitudes and peaceful habits are essential to leadership, and should be considered more constructive than any amount of wealth and force. Role modeling acceptance, tolerance, friendship, happiness, and other gentle strengths of humanity are great gifts to society.

When a person believes in himself or herself, his or her spirit becomes more open to new things that are good and healthy. We should strive to be thoughtful, reflective, and pensive people then, learning from history through memories and role models. Every day, everyone in the world should do at least one thing that is thoughtful and kind for others. Doing so can help each person believe in himself or herself more fully, and give confidence that may inspire each person to do more and more new and good things for themselves, for others, and for the world. Those positive attitudes and actions can be the first of many steps toward the journey for world peace.

ON BEING PRACTICAL Even when one individual or group prevails through some type of power over another, there is no real victory in violence or war. Any time there is loss, of life or land or reverence or resources, nobody really "wins." During the course of long-standing feuds or relentless battles, the very needs or rights being fought for are often destroyed, or even ignored or forgotten. That is one of the many reasons why we should be practical in making decisions about how to resolve conflict and ensure justice and peace.

Being practical means making sensible decisions and implementing constructive plans that are responsive to needs and desires, while simultaneously reflecting reasonable judgment and realistic ambitions. Being aware of and attentive to the unique and varied needs of people across cultures and environments and situations is essential to practical approaches. And, the prudent wisdom that leads to practical accords and resolutions requires knowledge that comes from both academic education and active involvement in local, community, and/or world organizations and activities.

The more we know about others, the more we understand about them, including things that are different from our own way of thinking and living. And the more we understand, the less we fear things we do not know about. When we are unsure about the facts and details of something, we often fill in the blanks using our own imaginations, or even ideas we have heard from others who may not know any more about the reality of a situation than we do. We could think of ourselves as little children, facing our first day of school, or some medical procedure that we have heard of but never experienced. When we are educated about what we may see, hear, and feel, and when we understand the necessity of the experience, we are better able to appreciate new things and more prepared to cope with adversity.

Some colleges and universities offer courses or programs in peace studies, but most elementary and high schools do not have "peace" as a subject. However, many schools educate children about the condition of war, and many offer lessons or activities encouraging mediation and nonviolent solutions to conflict. Some schools even support clubs and youth-oriented organizations that teach creative techniques for problem solving and conflict resolution so that children can develop habits that promote peace, such as boycotting, peaceful protesting, or campaigning.

Through information and community activities, children explore the importance of honest communication and interactions, which include active listening and sensitive responding to promote ongoing negotiation. For example, children practice objectively recounting an event that led to a problem, and saying what they need or feel by stating facts without judging the intent or character of another person. They also then practice listening to others respond to their words, discussing possible solutions, putting the chosen solution into action, evaluating the success of the plan, and even trying something new if that solution does not work.

When children and adults become educated and active in programs and organizations that advocate for the needs and rights of others in a peaceful and just way, they gain valuable insights and practical skills that prepare and enable them to make a positive difference in the world. It is good to talk with, or at least read about, people who are from countries and cultures and situations other than our own. When we get to know others through communication and education, we understand them as people who are very much like ourselves. The more we learn about others, the more we recognize our similarities and respect our differences, which leads to individuals and groups becoming a part of "us" rather than representing a group of "them." And when we are able to see the world as being filled with billions of us, and not groups of us and them, there is more understanding and acceptance, which leads to hope and peace.

It is important to recognize that in seeking justice and peace, we cannot merely assume a "one size fits all" approach and impose our personal preferences and standards on other people. Instead, we must be committed to learning about current events and situations, about cultural and ethnic diversity, and about environmental and economic variation that affects everything from agriculture to transportation and the availability of immunizations to technology. We must educate ourselves so we can integrate lessons from the past with hopes for the future and plans for the present, without telling others how they must run their government or how they must provide for their citizens.

On being poetic Being poetic is not necessarily synonymous with writing poetry. True, there are poetic people whose words, flowing through fingers or lips, are captured in some essence on paper or in minds. And some of these poets choose to create in free form, and some choose to work through various measures of rhyme or meter. But, there are also people who have the poetic qualities of being graceful and perceptive, aware and noticing, inspired and creative, and yet never pen a poem in their lifetime. Living life in a poetic way means being able to see familiar things in new ways. All people who live poetically, whether a particular verse ever results from such or not, choose to be observant and innovative, which are necessary attributes for peaceful attitudes and habits.

I have chosen to write poetry to help me cope with the many challenges of my personal life, and as a tool for reflecting on and responding to both the horrific tragedies and the glorious wonders of the world. For me, creating poetry is a positive way to release energy during times of anguish and of celebration, and a means to share my message of hope and peace with the world in a gently moving, yet credible and compelling, manner. There is something cathartic about sharing insights and aspirations. Even when a personal situation or worldwide dilemma cannot be imminently changed or resolved, trying to be a part of making a positive difference for someone, somewhere, sometime, just feels good.

Living life as a poet and in a poetic way means a willingness to try new things. One new thing I tried when I was younger was Hapkido, a Korean martial art. I have been asked by some people how I can be such a proponent for nonviolent conflict resolution, and yet also hold a First Degree Black Belt in martial arts. When I first began taking Hapkido at the age of four, the goals were for me to improve motor skills and learn some self-defense techniques. Because of my disability, I was very awkward and clumsy when walking or trying to run, and my speech was very slurred because of the tracheostomy tube that had been my connection to life support and breathing. And sadly, because I was "different" from other children, I was often left out and teased by many of them, and even the victim of physical bullying.

During my five years of training, I learned much more than how to control my body and balance, and how to defend myself and perform specific moves that are a part of Hapkido. By being open to what Hapkido really offered as an art, I also learned many life lessons, like how to remain peaceful in my body and in my spirit, even when it is hard to concentrate on being peaceful or optimistic. I learned manners, respect, patience, self-control, confidence, and many other important attributes to being a peaceful person. I learned to have confidence in my self and in my world, and I learned to defend myself if necessary but never to attack.

Through martial arts I achieved more than just personal lessons, colored belts, and trophies . . . I also learned to make new friends. Before studying Hapkido, I was unaware that these people existed. But through the course of my training, I met many people, and learned about people who lived on the other side of the world, and came to appreciate our common goals and interests, and to respect our cultural differences and ways of life.

Being open to new things, being observant and willing and flexible, are poetic qualities. I am committed to teaching peace to people around the world. I will do this by helping people understand what is important in life, including the need for balance and defense, but never violence or attack. Through my poetry and my words and my life, I want to teach by setting a good example, and by talking to others and sharing my ideas and words with them.

ON BEING PRAYERFUL For hope and peace to be real, we must believe in the goodness of people, of humanity, and of the future. And, if we choose to believe in a supreme being, we must believe in that as good, too. Many claim to be holy, or at least spiritual, people. We attend some service on some day of the week to "keep holy the Sabbath." But if we are truly holy or spiritual, then God, by whichever name we choose to call our creator, will be part of everything we say and do, on every day of the week. And in making this a reality, prayer becomes a strengthening thread that weaves through every aspect of our personal and professional "to-do" lists.

I try to be a good person, and I strive to be spiritual and prayerful. But I know that recognizing and appreciating God's presence is not always first on my "to-do" list. Sometimes, it's not there at all. God could, and should, be a part of all that I think, and all that I say, and all that I do. When I am choosing my words and actions, I should always consider the presence and goodness of God, instead of merely what meets my own needs and desires and pleases the needs and desires of others. God, by all names and faiths, is a part of our circle of life.

Being prayerful is not the same as being religious. Religion is about creeds and convictions, tenets and rituals, all of which serve to structure our beliefs and guide us through the joys and challenges of life. While there are many prayers specific to various religions, being a prayerful person need not be limited to or defined by any specific doctrine. Being prayerful is more about being hopeful and reflective, and trusting in the power of goodness.

We can pray with thoughts, with words, or with actions. We can pray alone, or with others. We can pray during celebrations and victories, and during challenges and disasters. We can even pray during the mundane routines of everyday life, like driving to work or doing chores or walking the dog. And, we should be prayerful during all moments of decision making, whether we are choosing an attitude or an action that will inevitably touch the world in some way.

I believe that all prayers are heard. But I also believe that prayers are not wishes, or commands, or if-then negotiations and promises between people and a supreme being. The process and power of prayer is really that of communication—an interaction between our minds and hearts and spirits and that of who we are praying to. God understands all languages, and the sounds that come from all anguish and all glory. In being prayerful, we are making a choice to hope, and hope is strengthening for all realities of life.

Responses to prayer, even miracles, occur in everyday life. We may miss many of them because we are seeking some different response or outcome.

I believe that being prayerful connects us to the goodness and presence of God, though, even during the most difficult of times. And, we must open our minds and hearts and spirits, and our eyes and ears and lives to the vast possibilities of responses from that to whom we pray. Even the silence of God can give us a calming strength, if we are seeking goodness and justness, and not merely gratification and justification.

There is nothing wrong with desires or seeking to have a prosperous life. We just need to be careful that in our pursuit of happiness and liberty and wealth and success, however we choose to define it, we are not overlooking the same pursuits by others. Trying to be a good person matters. But in the busyness of everyday life, we often neglect to be prayerful. All religions or moral approaches to life can lead us to be the good people we were created to be, and being prayerful is where peace and hope begin.

ON BEING PHILOSOPHICAL Deciding to face challenges with courage and optimism and to resolve conflicts using nonviolent methods is admirable. But sometimes, there are challenges that seem relentlessly overwhelming, and conflicts that seem to have no gentle solution. That is why choosing to have one or more personal philosophies to guide us through even the most difficult situations can be very helpful.

A philosophy is a motivational motto or proverbial slogan that reminds us about a particular point of view or way of thinking. Even when they seem cliché in banality, life philosophies can offer the wisdom and encouragement we need to get through the next moment, or day, or occurrence of whatever difficulty we are facing. It's like having a personal mantra that inspires us when we do not think we can persevere any longer.

I am particularly inspired by three life philosophies. The first is my own, which I initially realized when I was five years old: "Remember to play after every storm." There are many storms in life, some of them briefly intense, and some of them grueling and life-altering. A storm can be anything from the distress of trying to meet a deadline at school or work, to the devastating effects of a natural disaster on people and property, to the death of a family member or friend due to illness or disability. Life storms are inevitable, and they may come in infrequent or steady waves, or in sudden unpredictable tsunamis. My life philosophy reminds me that once I have gotten through whatever storm I have weathered, I must make time to play. I must rejuvenate my spirit, because it feels good to celebrate, and because in doing so I am strengthening my spirit for the next storm, which is sure to be a part of life. And when we make the effort to celebrate and play with others, we strengthen the circle of caring support for future storms.

Life is short, sweet, and sacred. That is why I am inspired by a second philosophy, which is the one my mom has chosen to guide her through challenges and conflict: "Celebrate life every day, in some way." If we do not have a reason, a desire, to find something good, something worthy, in some moment and person of each day, the trials and tribulations of life will become gravely crushing. Being sad or angry or miserable are natural responses to hardships, and sometimes they are the easiest emotions to display. But being sad or angry or miserable does not change a reality, or promote a positive source of strength that can help us through the hardship. Though it is sometimes a difficult task, choosing to rejoice in something, even something small and even during times that seem despairing, can remind us why we care about life, which is good.

The third philosophy that helps me when things are very difficult is the motto chosen by Jimmy Carter to guide him: "If you want something bad enough, never give up trying for it and you will succeed." This is an interesting and intriguing concept, because it does not imply that if we try hard enough we will eventually get what we want. Rather, it states that if we keep working toward a goal, we will be successful. And being successful can be broadly defined. It does not necessarily mean that we have reached our original goal, but that we have reached something worthy of our effort.

Having a philosophy is like hearing the song in our heart—our personal message that inspires us to become the best person we can be and to share whatever gifts we have with others. What we need and desire most in life are the gifts we should offer to others. More than one person can be motivated by the same philosophy, or many people can interpret one philosophy in various ways. But the value of having a philosophy is the perspective it can put on life, especially during difficult situations.

Being philosophical can remind us that when we are considering our challenges, if we have enough breath to complain about anything, then we have more than enough reason to give thanks about something.

ON BEING PURPOSEFUL It is said that "absence makes heart grow fonder." Perhaps it would be better if "presence made the heart grow fondest." I think we should each take time to consider our legacy—how we hope to be remembered in the future—and then consider what we are doing each day to make that a reality. Then, even when we have entered the eternity of our future through death, we can live in the present of our past, which is the essence we create in each today.

Living a life of purpose develops from choosing to be pensive and practical, poetic and philosophical, even prayerful, in resolving to make a positive difference in the world. Sometimes our legacy touches only one person in our immediate family, and sometimes our legacy will touch millions of people in future generations. But always, the fact that we were created and existed, for one minute or for 101 years, matters. Doing great and noble things does not always mean being powerful or internationally recognized or even living a life of many, many years. It means making a positive difference. And we can make it our mission to place meaning in all existence and to leave a positive impact on life as we touch it.

I was born into a life filled with personal challenges, and abundant with financial and medical and physical and emotional hardships. When people hear about my life, they hear a story filled with words that detail disability, divorce, even death—of my siblings, of my friends, and perhaps soon, of my own body. And after hearing bits of my story, I am often asked how I can find so much positive energy, happiness, and satisfaction in such a difficult life. The simple answer is that I have chosen to live my life with optimism, seeking and embracing opportunities for growth and change and fellowship and strength, for myself, and for the world.

Sometimes, by chance I am able to bridge from a hindering obstacle to a facilitating possibility. And sometimes, by choice, I force myself to rely on attitudes and habits I have developed that foster resiliency and get me into my next moment. Not all chances and choices are truly beneficial in the end, but all opportunities are worthy of inquiry. And like studying history, there is valuable knowledge to be gained from lessons of opportunity, as we learn from the struggles and successes and even the failures of people and events both in history and today.

When I die, I want to be remembered as "a poet, a peacemaker, and a philosopher who played." And so, I feel blessed to be living with a purpose, and I try to do what I can each day to create that legacy. I seek peace in my own life and for my own spirit. And I seek ways to use my words and experiences to share peaceful thoughts and ideas with others, so that we can all live in justice and peace. I embrace opportunities to try and gently remind people about what was, what is, and what could be, for our world, if we make peace something that really matters.

I believe that we are able to touch the future, because we are creating history in each moment of our present. I believe that in being purposeful, we should celebrate each new year, each new day, each new moment, remembering the past, but not dwelling in it. We should fully use the present, but not waste it. We should live for the future, but not count on it. We should appreciate and rejoice that we have each new moment, day, and year. Every life, whether filled with burdens or blessings, challenges or opportunities, disasters or dreams come true, can be affected by chosen attitudes and habits. And we can each choose to live with a purpose, realizing that our choices in how we think, speak, and act today, will create the epitaph and legacy of our lives—the echo and silhouette of our essence in the future.

ON BEING PEACEFUL One of the many goals of the United Nations is to develop friendships among all nations, and to promote social justice so that all people in the world can live a good life. And certainly, one of the things the world could use most is a harmonic, eternal friendship, within and between all people. Developing friendships among individuals, families, neighbors, communities, countries, and nations is a simple, yet profound, concept. Imagine a world at peace, where we are all united in friendship . . . each hand of each person joined in another, like a giant river of peace.

International friendship could begin with just two people who are true friends, with two groups who are mutually respectful, with two countries that are collectively committed to equity and justice . . . then flow out to others, flooding the world with hope and commitment. When one person is thoughtful to another, the thoughtfulness gets carried on. It is like a river of kindness, once blocked by rocks, that is suddenly opened by a single person's kind thought or act. The river runs freely again, and continues to flow, moving more rocks and reaching, touching the hearts of others, with more kindness. This kindness can flow stronger and stronger, expanding from small streams within neighborhoods to rivers of thoughtfulness growing through districts, states, countries, and even continents. Soon, we could have a whole ocean of friendships.

Being peaceful is being a part of the river of kindness. It is being nonviolent, and working with others collaboratively. It is being pleasant and friendly, and it relies on trust and honesty and respect and humility. It involves thinking respectfully about others, speaking considerately, and acting in ways that encourage others to be peaceful as well. Being peaceful is a choice.

Not being peaceful is a choice, too. When we are selfish, or defiant, or unkind, we are choosing to not be peaceful. And there will always be times when we are frustrated and then think, or say, or do, something that we regret later. But the great thing about friendship is that we can also say that we are sorry when we are selfish or make a mistake. And because we have a relationship based on honesty and trust, we can be forgiven and the river of kindness can continue to flow.

In being peaceful, we realize that when mistakes are made, we reconcile through forgiveness and collaboration. In being peaceful, we do not correct mistakes or seek restitution through revenge, or retaliation, or through committing another mistake. The Golden Rule reminds us of the essential philosophy to guide friendships: "Do unto others as you would have them do unto you." This age-old proverb does not state that we should do unto others as they have done to us, but as we would have, or want, them to unto us. The river of kindness that fosters friendship, and world peace, flows with mercy, not vengeance.

JUST PEACE

Our world today has many problems. While our world is filled with natural resources and beauty, we have pollution that puts animals, plants, land, water, air, and even humans in danger. While our world is filled with billions of good and generous people, we are also facing the problem of a world that lacks respect—respect for self and respect for others and respect for the earth. While our world is filled with water and food and medicine, there is the problem of too many people who are thirsty and hungry and dying because we have not equitably distributed provisions for these basic needs. And one of the worst problems in the world, and one that is avoidable, are the issues of violence and hatred and intolerance that lead to war.

The terrorist acts that continue to exist in our world today are dreadful. They are horrific, devastating, and unacceptable. But we cannot continue to judge groups of people by the violent acts of individuals, and we cannot continue to judge cultures and countries by the violent acts of some groups and sects. Nor can we continue to repeat these acts of terror in attempts of retaliation or revenge, or even in attempts to rid the world of injustice and to secure peace.

While we must battle the issue of terrorism, the war against terror cannot ever be won through a wealth of weapons or through the stealth of armies. The problem of terrorism can only be solved through the equitable provision of basic necessities to all people, through the collective commitment of all people to nonviolent conflict resolution, and through the veracity of tolerance and mutual respect for the unique differences and preferences that are inevitable, and necessary, between and among groups of people throughout the world.

I have chosen to seek and endeavor a plan for peace in a world where conflict has always existed, and where conflict will inevitably continue to exist. I have learned that there are all different types of peace, such as inner peace, and peace between individuals, and peace among nations, and peace with the earth on which we live. I have even come to accept that there will be people who will claim that the quickest and most effective path to peace is violence and war.

And while I realize that there is no guarantee that a particular nonviolent method of problem solving will work in all places or in all situations, I will reaffirm my commitment to seeking peaceful resolutions for all conflict, because violence only leads to more violence. Equitable solutions and change come through collaboration, not conquering. Peace is possible, because peace begins with an attitude, and an attitude is a choice. And I have chosen to do what I believe I am here for, during my brief time on earth—to share a message of hope and peace with the world. A message of hope and peace. Just peace.

Mattie delivering a speech about "peace beginning with being OK with who you are as a person, and having hope for the future," December 2003.

Mattie signing Heartsong bookplates, January, 2004, to be used as gifts and fund-raising incentives in his final two books.

For Our World

We need to stop.
Just stop.
Stop for a moment . . .
Before anybody
Says or does anything
That may hurt anyone else.
We need to be silent.
Just silent.
Silent for a moment . . .
Before we forever lose
The blessing of songs
That grow in our hearts.
We need to notice.
Just notice.
Notice for a moment . . .
Before the future slips away
Into ashes and dust of humility.

Stop, be silent, and notice . . .
In so many ways, we are the same.
Our differences are unique treasures.
We have, we are, a mosaic of gifts
To nurture, to offer, to accept.
We need to be.
Just be.
Be for a moment . . .
Kind and gentle, innocent and trusting,
Like children and lambs,
Never judging or vengeful
Like the judging and vengeful.
And now, let us pray,
Differently, yet together,
Before there is no earth, no life,
No chance for peace.

By Mattie J.T. Stepanek, September 11, 2001,
in Hope Through Heartsongs
(Hyperion/VSP, 2002)

E-mail from: Jimmy Carter
Date: January 16, 2004 7:36 AM EST
To: Mattie J.T. Stepanek
Subject: (no subject)

To Jeni: I will cooperate with Mattie on the book, and will be glad to be interviewed. Give him my love, confidence, and encouragement.

Jimmy

E-mail from: Jeni Stepanek
Date: January 22, 2004
To: Jimmy Carter
Subject: Message from Mattie

Dear Jimmy,
[Mattie is in a lot of pain and is unable to e-mail right now, but he wanted me to convey the following information to you . . .]
     Yesterday, Mattie came home from the ICU again. He will have to go to the hospital every other day for platelet and blood transfusions, and he is still quite fragile. He knows and understands that his body is dying, and that there is not really anything anyone can do to stop the process. We can, however, (or it seems) slow the process with all the IV fluids and blood products. He is anticipating getting through this really bad cycle/progression, and then looking better again. But he knows that he will "look" better because he is on continuous IV fluids and blood products. That means that when the disease progresses again, depending on how severe the cycle is, it could be the final one as we would not have additional support available since he's already on so much. It's not what he would choose for his future, but he accepts it as his future, and chooses to LIVE until death, rather than spend the time dying until death occurs. He knows, realistically, he could live a couple of weeks, or if it's meant to be, he could live a couple of years. He's just playing after (and even during) the storms, and celebrating life, and staying determined. He wants to thank you for being such a good friend to him, and he looks forward to making the "Just Peace" project a reality.
     You are a true inspiration as a peacemaker, as a friend, as a person. Every parent's dream is for their child to be happy and healthy. So I thank you for your part in making my child happy, and spiritually healthy.

With deep respect, and love from Mattie,
Jeni Stepanek

E-mail from: Jimmy Carter
Date: January 23, 2004 7:97 AM EST
To: Mattie J.T. Stepanek
Subject: (no subject)

Jeni: . . . I have made the final decision. As work on the book progresses, Mattie just needs to let me know how I can be of help. Give him my love.

Jimmy

E-mail from: Jimmy Carter
Date: June 22, 2004 5:25 PM EST
To: Jeni Stepanek
Subject: Mattie

To Jeni:
We are deeply saddened by the passing of our young friend. Mattie has touched us personally and deeply, and our lives have been expanded by having known him. A hero in the truest sense, he has inspired countless people with his indomitable spirit and constant quest for peace. Please know that you remain in our hearts and prayers. We trust that your faith, courage, and warm memories will be of comfort to you in this time of loss.

With love,
Jimmy and Rosalynn Carter

Mattie's friend, Hope Wyatt, and her mother Susan Wyatt have created, painted, and assembled thousands of "Sunset Memorial Ribbons of Hope" to honor Mattie's message and to benefit the MDA Mattie Fund.

Choice Lesson

Growth brings change.
Unpredictable change,
Which can bring
Hesitancy to optimism.
It is essential that we cope
With the realities of the past
And the uncertainties of the future
With a pure and chosen hope.
Not a blind faith,
But a strengthened choice.
Then, we can have the
Fortitude and wisdom necessary
To integrate life's many lessons
That collect beyond points in time.
Growing like this will help
Build a good future,
For individuals,
For communities,
And for the world.

By Mattie J.T. Stepanek, February 18,
2000, in *Hope Through Heartsongs*
(Hyperion/VSP, 2001)

Forthword

BY JIMMY CARTER

For any fortunate reader who has been inspired by this book, it is natural to ask a crucial question: Where do we go from here? The author knew the answer, and through his poems, letters, and essays, he has found an innovative way to lead us there.

The *Forthword* itself is one of the unprecedented contributions that Mattie Stepanek has made to help us take the next step. It was his dream that the encapsulation of his ideas and poetry into one volume would not represent the final achievement of his influential life, but rather that it would launch his spirit into the future. It is inevitable that we would be both amazed and touched by the simultaneous simplicity and profundity of the basic message that has risen from this small boy's heart.

More than anyone else I've ever known, he has been able to comprehend his own inner feelings, to extrapolate them with a unique resonance for the understanding of other people, and then to embrace in his brilliant mind the challenges and opportunities of the entire world. This is an amazing, almost an inconceivable aptitude—unless you happened to know Mattie Stepanek.

In brief moments of inspiration, most of us have had flashes of insight, with transient concepts of what we and others together might do to bring an end to the sources of suffering and despair that we human beings have wrought. For Mattie, this period of inspiration encompassed his entire life, and his ability to articulate his ideas with such clarity and beauty has affected me deeply and changed my life, along with the lives of millions of others who loved and admired this remarkable young boy.

A natural question for most people, including famous or influential leaders, is how we can really make a difference. I remember a cartoon drawn by a volunteer for Habitat for Humanity that made a great impression on me. I have included the same description in my most recent book.

It was a panorama of a village, maybe from an airplane flying over-head. Some people are playing tennis, some are riding bicycles, others are in automobiles, teaching school, maybe some plowing tractors, and a little thought bubble above each one's head says, "What can just one person do?" It becomes obvious that, when combined, the small, individual con-tributors of caring, friendship, forgiveness, and love—each of us different from our next door neighbors—can form a phalanx, an army, with almost unlimited capability.

What we can do individually is adopt Mattie's apparently naive commit-ment to a coalescence of the finest human traits, including peace, justice, equity, humility, service, compassion, and love. Abbreviating these, he advocated "just peace" being the guiding principle in our relationships with *all* other people, and the focus of our involvement in the religious, ethical, and political environments in which we live. He thought that each of us should pause for a few moments now and then and plan what we might do to promote a just peace, setting our goals as high as possible. He wanted us to respect ourselves, first of all, and then to respect all other people.

There have been a few times during my life when I had a large audience, and I attempted to express my primary concerns and hopes as clearly and succinctly as possible. One of these occasions was my inaugural address as president, when I described how I would contribute directly as the leader of a powerful nation in the promotion of human rights. A quarter century later, I had another opportunity when I received the Nobel Prize for Peace. I have hoped that there would be some permanent impact of these presentations.

Immediately after my Nobel lecture in Oslo, I walked outside to a near-by hill and found a small stone that I brought back for Mattie, because I had incorporated into my remarks some of the ideas that he had shared with me in our treasured personal conversations. Perhaps the most significant of Mattie's many suggestions were in this closing passage:

> War may sometimes be a necessary evil. But no matter how neces-sary, it is always an evil, never a good. We will not learn how to live together in peace by killing each other's children.

> The bond of our common humanity is stronger than the divisive-
> ness of our fears and prejudices. God gives us the capacity for choice.
> We can choose to alleviate suffering. We can choose to work together
> for peace. We can make these changes—and we must.

This was my best attempt to craft the words. I'm sure that Mattie could have done it more beautifully. But he has chosen a different forum. With this book, he has taken the opportunity to plant multiple seeds in the minds and hearts of all his readers, with the expectation that each one of us would make a personal commitment to a just peace.

If we heed Mattie's message, then we know where to go from here. Sharing his vision, we will follow the path prepared for us by this special child of God, and we will continue his journey together.

"My Step, My Choice, My Journey Forth," artwork by Mattie, September 1998.

The Message

There can never be
Too many odes to the morning,
When the birth'ing of dawn
Reflects rainbow reversals . . .
Orange-star-guide rising
Into cerulean skies so gently
That it caresses downy offerings,
Highlighting horizons
　　At 'east in the heavens.

There can never be
Too many songs of an evening,
When the dusk'ing of days
Echoes shell silhouettes . . .
Dragon-cloud-wisps scaling
Azure skies so bright with darkness
That it grays into black,
Twilighting yesterviews
　　Toward western welkin.

There can never be
Too many hopes in each moment,
When the real'izing of truth
Resonates shadow directions . . .
Gold-etched-treasures billowing
Cirrus or cumulus so boldly into skies
That it lifts setting stains of yore,
Hindsight-edging sleepy darkness
　　From earthen eyes.

There can never be
Too many elegies for our living,
When the wake'ing of souls
Invites celestial cycles . . . .
Baby-blanket-beginnings fading, folding
Ephemeral pink-white-blue skies into
The stillness of age so nurtured into
Foresighting firmament,
  Paths of possibilities—

  . . . Oh, the skies of insight,
  Open eyes of wisdom—
  Our daily gifts,
  Guiding, guarding, granting, giving
  Resolution and revelation into future,
  As we grow and be and rest
    In just peace.

By Mattie J.T. Stepanek, October 15, 2003,
for *Just Peace: A Message of Hope*
(Andrews McMeel Publishing, 2006)

Appendices

Yes, hope is a garden
Grown from love and from tears,
And hope which is nurtured
Survives throughout years.

Excerpt from "About Hope," May 21, 2003,
by Mattie J.T. Stepanek, in *Reflections of a Peacemaker:
A Portrait Through Heartsongs*
(Andrews McMeel Publishing, 2005)

JIMMY CARTER: PEANUT FARMER, POLITICIAN, AND PEACEMAKER

BY MATTIE STEPANEK, SPRING 1998

James Earl Carter Jr. was born in 1924. He grew up in a small farming town called Plains, in the state of Georgia. During his life, "Jimmy" has worked on his family's farm, studied law, and helped people all over the world. His parents, James Earl Carter Sr. and "Miss Lillian" Carter, probably never thought that their son would grow up to be a famous peanut farmer, politician, and peacemaker.

JIMMY CARTER—PEANUT FARMER

When Jimmy Carter was a child, he helped run his family's peanut farm. He helped plow the fields using mules. He also cut wood, stacked peanut vines, fed chickens, and mended fences. In his free time, Jimmy liked to run, jump, swim, and ride horses. In high school and college, he played basketball, football, and tennis, and he ran cross-country track. He attended many different schools and churches.

When he was six years old, Jimmy decided to go into the peanut business himself. He waited until there were about fifty peanuts growing on an underground vine. Then, he pulled up the peanut plant, and loaded his wagon with the nuts. He took them home, soaked them overnight and boiled them in salt water. Every Saturday, he'd sell about 20 small bags of peanuts for a nickel each. He never went home until he had sold every single bag. To this day, Jimmy Carter says that fresh boiled peanuts are much better than roasted peanuts that people buy in a store.

As he got older, Jimmy wanted to be a navy submarine soldier. He stopped wanting to be this when an admiral was having a meeting with him and his class team at the Naval Academy. The admiral asked Jimmy if he had always tried his best while he was at school. Jimmy started to say "yes," but decided to be honest and say "no" because there were times he knew he could have tried harder. Then the admiral asked him "why" he hadn't always tried his best. This made Jimmy stop and really think about what he was doing with his life. He left the room and decided to study law and become a politician.

JIMMY CARTER—POLITICIAN

Jimmy Carter was elected governor of Georgia in 1970. He was very excited and surprised about his victory because he had lost the race for governor before. As governor, he made the state government work better. He got people of all races to work together, and to use mediation instead of anger to deal with problems.

In the 1970s, he told his mother, Miss Lillian, that he wanted to run for president of the United States of America. She was lying down, and he had propped his feet up on her bed. His mother looked at him for a long time, then said, "Jimmy, take your feet off my bed." That meant she thought it was a crazy idea, but she would support him. Jimmy Carter was elected our thirty-ninth president in 1976, and took office on January 20, 1977. On the morning after election day, Jimmy Carter said: "I see the sun rising on a new day, a beautiful spirit in the country . . . a commitment to the future."

While he was president, Jimmy Carter wanted to be a "man of the people." He liked to use his nickname, Jimmy, instead of his whole formal name. He also liked to dress casually, and usually wore sweaters instead of neat suits with button-down shirts and neckties. When he traveled, he liked to stay in ordinary people's homes instead of fancy hotels. He and his wife, Rosalynn Carter, and their nine-year-old daughter, Amy, chose to walk hand-in-hand from the Capitol to the White House on his Inauguration Day, instead of riding in a fancy limousine. (His other three children were grown-up).

Jimmy Carter wanted to change the way governments were run in our country and around the world. He thought that governments should not abuse citizens, even if they were communists, so he cut off relationships with communist countries that were not good to the citizens. While Jimmy Carter was president, oil prices kept getting higher. So Jimmy talked people into building smaller cars, then talked the citizens into buying the smaller cars.

This helped save money and the amount of gas our country used.

Jimmy Carter's biggest success as president was getting people from different countries to sign peace treaties and accords. Egypt and Israel were fighting. He invited leaders from these countries to Camp David. Camp David was where presidents went to rest and hang out. But Jimmy Carter used Camp David as a peaceful place in the mountains for leaders to talk about peace in the world. He got Egypt and Israel to sign a peace accord on September 17, 1978. It didn't solve everything, but it brought a little more peace and hope to those countries. He also worked on peace agreements between the Soviet Union (now Russia) and the United States.

JIMMY CARTER—PEACEMAKER

Although he lost when he ran for a second term, Jimmy Carter was a very good and peaceful president. He will be remembered by many people as a man who said we should "advocate for life, liberty, and the pursuit of happiness not just for ourselves, but for others." He said that the existence of war makes it impossible for people to have their basic needs met. Since he stopped being the president in January of 1981, Jimmy has done many things to continue his goal of world peace. He has helped stop war, he has helped homeless people find shelter, and he has set up organizations that help children and grown-ups who want to learn peace.

When Jimmy was little, his father believed in segregation. That means that his father thought that people who were black were not equal to people who were white, so they should not be allowed in the same places. So when black people would come to Jimmy's house, his father talked to them outside instead of letting them inside. Jimmy and his mother did not like this at all. They did not believe in segregation. They believed that people were equal no matter what their skin color was, and no matter what religion they were or what country they came from. Jimmy knew that when he grew up, he would try to change the way people thought about each other, so that everybody would know and believe that everybody was equal. Jimmy Carter is famous for saying: "If you have got any hatred left in your heart, get down on your knees and pray."

Jimmy Carter has been very active in helping people all over the world who need a place to live. He and his wife, Rosalynn, have worked with something called Habitat for Humanity since 1976. Habitat for Humanity was created in the 1940s by Miller and Linda Fuller. It was established to build houses for the homeless, first in Plains, Georgia, then in Zaire. Now, it serves people all over the United States and the world.

In Habitat for Humanity, people aren't just given free homes. Instead, they work side by side with other people in need to build or renovate (rebuild) homes. It is not charity or government funded. People donate services and time to building their own home, and then to building homes for other people who also need shelter. Jimmy Carter helps with this program by building houses. He also helps with other programs that try to make sure people have food, health care, education, and jobs.

Jimmy Carter helped set up the Carter Center. This is a private, nonprofit (not trying to make money) organization in Georgia, near the Presidential Library. It has lots of information for all people who need, or want to know about, education, health, the environment, human rights, civil rights, and global conflict and mediation. Anybody who wants to get information can use the Carter Center. It is for all people, from all religions, races, countries, and economic backgrounds (people who are rich and poor and in-between). People can go there to seek peaceful resolutions to troubling and complicated problems.

JIMMY CARTER—PLANS FOR THE FUTURE

Jimmy Carter believes that children and young people have rights, too, and that they are the future. He says that the pressures on children today are very different from pressures children had years ago. Families are different now, and there is more divorce. Also, there are more drugs, wars, and diseases like AIDS that children have to worry about. Jimmy Carter tries to encourage children to be aware, and to be involved in today's politics, because they are the future of the world. These are some of the things Jimmy Carter encourages young people to do, so that they are prepared for the future:

- Read as much as possible about what is happening in your community, your country, and the world.
- Promote peace by sharing concerns with others, during family meals to town council meetings.
- Reflect and think about all the things you learn each day. Keep a journal and notes about what's happening in your world, and about how you feel about events.
- Be prepared to vote. Be informed all your life so you are ready and can make good choices.
- Support mediation, and peaceful conflict resolution, instead of arguments and violence.
- Be involved in family, community, and world events. For example, work with the Big Brothers program or Habitat for Humanity.
- Be an active part of building the future.

JIMMY CARTER—A PERFECT HERO

I really liked doing this report on Jimmy Carter. He is one of my heroes, and a role model for my life now, and for my future. When I grow up, I would like to be a peacemaker, just like Jimmy Carter. But instead of being a president, I would like to do it by being a writer. Like Jimmy Carter, I want to travel to different countries and talk about the importance of peace.

Jimmy Carter and I have some other things in common, too. We both love the song "Amazing Grace." Both of us love to read, and our favorite gift to receive is a book. We both love pancakes, cornbread, fruit, and vegetables. But Jimmy Carter's favorite meat is steak, and mine is ribs. We both like sports, but mine is martial arts, and his are basketball, football, and tennis. We both love to watch baseball games. Best of all, we both like to talk about God, and we both hope for a better future. We both believe that children are an important part of the future and that their rights should always be respected and protected.

Nobel Peace Letter and Rock from Jimmy Carter

JIMMY CARTER

17 December 2002

To Mattie Stepanek

    After I received the Nobel Peace prize, I walked out of the City Hall, climbed a small adjacent hill overlooking the sea, and found this rock. Nearby was an ancient castle, a statue of Franklin D. Roosevelt, and a memorial sculpture that I helped dedicate in 1995 to the Norwegian people for their work in bringing peace to the Middle East.

    I felt that you were with me in spirit.

Love,

Jimmy Carter

Nobel Site
Oslo, Norway
12/10/02

MDA QUEST Article

REPRINT FROM MDA MAGAZINE QUEST,
VOLUME II, NUMBER I, JANUARY/FEBRUARY 2004

BY TARA WOOD

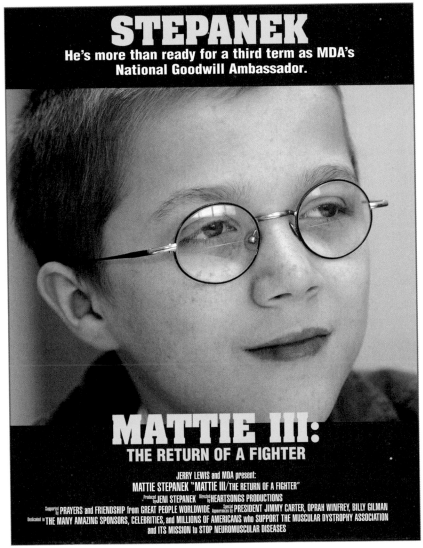

Muscular Dystrophy Association poster created to celebrate Mattie's third term as MDA National Goodwill Ambassador in 2004.

He's revved up and ready. . . .

He's making up for lost time. . . .

He's determined to make a difference in the world. . . .

Sound like a movie trailer for an upcoming thriller?

Actually, "he" is Mattie Stepanek, and this hype is about how the thirteen-year-old from Maryland is eagerly taking on his third term as MDA National Goodwill Ambassador.

Although he may not be fighting aliens or evil bad guys like an action movie star, Mattie's three years of service as MDA National Goodwill Ambassador could be loosely compared to a hit Hollywood trilogy:

- *Mattie* (the original): A smash hit that topped the charts.
- *Mattie II*: Same outstanding lead character and great promise, but gets bogged down by timing problems.
- *Mattie III*: Expectations are high for another blockbuster.

In fact, nobody has higher expectations than Mattie himself as he readies to represent MDA at a variety of local and national events this year.

Mattie is known worldwide for his best-selling "Heartsongs" poetry books and peacemaking efforts. He's also making a name for his incredible history of fighting back from serious complications of his neuromuscular disease.

Mattie has mitochondrial myopathy, which causes muscle weakness and difficulty regulating body functions such as heart rate. His mother, Jeni, is affected by an adult-onset form of the disease, and Mattie's three older siblings died from it.

READY FOR ANOTHER ROUND

Mattie was ecstatic—and uncharacteristically speechless—when MDA officials asked him to serve a third term, a request that hasn't been made since the 1960s.

"When I first got the phone call, I didn't know what to say. It was one of the few, rare times that I quit talking. It was just such a shocking surprise," Mattie said.

Looking back at his second term in 2003, Mattie said he's most affected by the things he was forced to miss because of a four-month stay at Children's Hospital in Washington, D.C.

"I was really disappointed, not about what I did do, but what I didn't do," he said.

From February to May, Mattie was treated for a bleeding airway, a situation that at times was very grave. The experience was similar to a downturn in 2001 that saw him on the brink of death.

Mattie then, too, made what doctors called a "miraculous" recovery, and soon afterwards he vaulted into the national spotlight as the nation was captivated by his poetry, wisdom, and message of peace and understanding.

This year, rotten timing of health complications forced him to miss some of his favorite MDA events, such as the Ride for Life, a huge gathering of East Coast Harley-Davidson enthusiasts that has raised millions for MDA.

Instead, he found himself "just sitting there bleeding and coughing every day, and the doctors saying, 'He might die,'" Mattie said.

After two weeks in the hospital, Mattie was released temporarily to attend the first annual Heartsongs Gala in Washington, an MDA benefit that honored Mattie's spirit and his life philosophy of "playing after every storm."

The February event coincided with the release of his fifth book, *Loving Through Heartsongs*, and a massive snowstorm on the East Coast that snowed in many guests and friends who attended the gala.

Mattie said he and Jeni made the most of his time out of the hospital by ordering pizza, spending time with friends, and attempting a snowball fight with the "yucky" city snow.

The highly successful gala and the blizzard helped keep his mind off his pending return to the hospital and the seriousness of his situation.

"I was so nervous because I knew this could probably be either the last two days I'd see the outside world for a really long time, or the last two days I'd see the outside world ever," he said.

THE COMEBACK KID

But Mattie is Mattie, and he found his way out of the hospital in May, just in time to attend a weeklong MDA summer camp and celebrate his thirteenth birthday on July 17. He marked the milestone with a big crab feast he'd been planning for years, he said.

The year also included an exciting collaboration with teenage recording artist Billy Gilman, now MDA's National Youth Chairperson. Gilman's album *Music Through Heartsongs: Songs Based on the Poems of Mattie J.T. Stepanek* was released in April.

Mattie also cites the 2003 Jerry Lewis MDA Telethon as a terrific highlight of the year.

Unable to travel to Los Angeles because of his fragile health, Mattie appeared on the national broadcast live via satellite from Baltimore. But by no means did he take it easy on Labor Day weekend.

He also co-emceed the local broadcast with Bruce Cunningham, a Baltimore sports anchor with Fox-45 News, for twenty-one hours straight, and helped set a new record for pledges raised.

At times the broadcast was very emotional for him, particularly when a segment honored a friend who had passed away during MDA Summer Camp.

Mattie told viewers, "This is what we're fighting for, it's to prevent things like this from happening. No one who is going to camp, which is a week of heaven—to celebrate life, and heaven on earth—should go to the real heaven during that week."

BACK TO A "NORMAL" LIFE

Nowadays, the Stepaneks are grateful to have a "typical" week whenever they can. That means tending to Mattie's ongoing homeschooling by Jeni and Jeni's graduate work at the University of Maryland.

A new medical protocol also occupies much of his time, as Mattie goes to the hospital weekly on an outpatient basis for transfusions of platelets and sometimes red blood cells.

Last year, doctors realized that the frequent transfusions were causing an iron overload in his blood, so he now undergoes regular treatments with

Desferal (deferoxamine mesylate) to reduce the iron level and protect his liver. He has to watch for side effects from the drug, including low blood pressure.

"It seems that every time we jump one hurdle, another one comes out of nowhere," said Mattie, who has a crystal-clear grasp of his health status, right down to reciting what his vital signs and the levels of iron, oxygen, and other chemicals in his blood should be.

"It's very important that I know in case there's an emergency and I'm the only one to answer questions," Mattie said, adding that he likes to be involved in his care. "I like to know what's going on, why it's going on, and how it happens, how long it takes, things like that. In fact, once I'm in tune, I like to help out."

Despite the ups and downs of his health struggle, Mattie continues to welcome and firmly embrace the events of everyday life.

MORE SCHOOL, MORE WRITING

QUEST interviewed Mattie on a test day, with history and English emerging as his favorite school subjects. He also enjoys taking part in monthly events for the local MDA teen club, chess lessons, and giving lots of love to his service dog-in-training, Micah.

Mattie's fans will notice that his boyish grin is giving way to the mug of a maturing young man, and some faint but classic trademarks of a teenager can now be detected. Sprinkled lightly among his wise-beyond-his-years, philosophical conversation are words like "cool" and a laugh about how messy his room is.

"I'm keeping up my spirits. In fact, the only thing that's going wrong right now is my room needs cleaning. I'm looking at my bed and I'm thinking 'oh my gosh.'"

But again, Mattie is Mattie, and that means he's undertaking a new schedule of book signings and public speaking engagements.

In October he was honored by the U.S. Department of Health & Human Services for his humanitarian endeavors.

He's in the early stages of writing a book about peace, and plans for the second annual Heartsongs Gala (February 21) are in full swing. Of course, there are always other projects and ideas brewing.

Aside from the difficult times, Mattie says of 2003 that he is "glad I got to do what I did, and I'm going to keep doing."

Mattie and his team of supporters are taking extra precautions medically so that he can accomplish everything he hopes to this year.

He's also deeply grateful for the massive outpouring of help and good wishes he receives.

"One of the biggest reasons I keep pulling through is prayer and friendship," Mattie said, adding that on some days during his hospitalization it was hard to remain positive.

"Some days I would be furious, and I would say, 'I'm just going to give up. Come on, trachea, collapse.' The next day, I would say, 'I must have looked and sounded so stupid. I can't believe I did that.'"

Now, Mattie emphasizes, whether he's telling MDA sponsors and supporters or telling himself, it has never, ever been more important to keep fighting.

"It's important not to give up, and that's what MDA is about," he said.

MDA Ross Report

E-mail from: Bob Ross, President, Muscular Dystrophy Association
Date: June 23, 2004
To: Jeni Stepanek
Subject: "Ross Report" on the MDA Web site

MEMORIES OF MATTIE

MDA National Goodwill Ambassador Mattie Stepanek died yesterday at Children's Hospital in Washington, D.C., from complications of the mitochondrial muscular disorder that had affected him since early childhood. Mattie would have been fourteen on July 17.

Many things need to be said about this extraordinary young man, whose life and spirit had an immeasurably powerful impact on all of us at MDA, as well as on everyone who came to know him through his beautiful "Heartsongs" series of poetry books and his memorable television appearances.

First, our thoughts must turn to Mattie's mother, Jeni. At times, it seemed Mattie and his mom were so close they must have shared one soul between them. But the reality is that Jeni must go on without Mattie, as she had to go on after the loss of his three siblings to the same disease.

Although the death of Mattie, after several years of life-threatening medical crises, wasn't completely unexpected, the reality of the moment is still hard to endure for all of us who loved him. For Jeni, it must be hardest of all. All of us in the MDA family extend to her our love and deepest sympathy on this inconceivable loss.

MDA President Bob Ross proudly sharing his "wallet-sized Mattie photo."

The first occasion I had to write about Mattie in this column was in August 2000, before Mattie was a best-selling author or a national celebrity. I used that opportunity to reproduce an exquisite essay Mattie wrote about his experiences at MDA Summer Camp at Camp Maria in Leonardtown, Maryland [see page 179].

MDA Summer Camp is under way this week at Camp Maria and I know Mattie will be foremost in the thoughts of friends such as fellow camper Erin Kiernan, and MDA

Health Care Services Coordinators Katie McGuire and Annie Kennedy, and the rest of MDA's local office staff in the Baltimore/Washington area.

Mattie's legacy will be a rich one—preserved in the books he left us—and in the memories we'll all carry of him.

Some random memories of my own:

Mattie respectfully referring to International Association of Fire Fighters General President Harold Schaitberger as "Mr. Harold" on the 2001 national broadcast of the Telethon . . . the poem that Telethon anchor Ed McMahon, inspired by Mattie, wrote and read on the same Telethon . . . Mattie's look of shocked amazement, transforming to joy, when he received a surprise visit from his hero and role model, former President Jimmy Carter, on a segment of *Good Morning America* . . . Mattie sporting a pair of Larry King–style suspenders when he appeared on the famed talk show host's program on CNN . . . and Oprah Winfrey arranging for Mattie to meet the stars of the "Harry Potter" movie series on the set of her show.

I'll also remember Mattie, in his healthier, happier days, zipping around the backstage area of the 2002 Telethon in his motorized wheelchair, sometimes exasperating his mother, who wanted him to conserve his energy, but having a hell of a time, nonetheless.

Perhaps the moment that will stay with me most was when MDA National Chairman Jerry Lewis broke with a tradition of over three decades and, for the first and only time, sang his signature closing tune, "You'll Never Walk Alone," directly to one of "his kids," Mattie.

I'll also remember the many things Mattie loved: video games, his service dog, Micah, practical jokes, "Austin Powers" movies, *Yu-Gi-Oh!* trading cards, the Beatles, and numerous books from *The Lord of the Rings* to *Moby Dick*.

Mattie *didn't* love the seemingly endless weeks and months he spent at D.C. Children's Hospital, mostly because it meant he was unable to spread his message of peace and do the work he felt he had to do. But he *did* love the people who took care of him there and who loved him in return.

Mattie did love speaking to people. Whether he was addressing a huge crowd at an MDA "Heartsongs" gala in Washington or an MDA sponsor gathering . . . hanging out with his Harley-Davidson buddies at a Ride for Life in Pennsylvania . . . reading poems to admiring fans at one of his popular book signings . . . bonding with his close friend, singer and MDA National Youth Chairman Billy Gilman . . . or joking around with our MDA TV crew who came into his home in Maryland to videotape Mattie's profile for the Telethon . . . Mattie was a compelling and unfailingly optimistic ambassador, not just for MDA, but for the human spirit.

I won't forget that Mattie genuinely believed in peace . . . not just as a concept but as potential reality for our world. And, with similar depth of conviction, he believed that a medical answer would be found for the disease that affected him and his siblings, indeed for all of the children and adults fighting neuromuscular diseases. He knew that answer might not come in his own time. But he had unshakable faith that it would come, if we believed in it and worked to make it a reality.

Here's to Mattie Stepanek, and love and peace.

With every best wish . . .
Bob Ross
MDA President and CEO

Mattie's "All Hail the Sacred Monkey" tradition is being carried on at Camp Maria by his friends, and even new-comers to MDA Summer Camp. During the opening night campfire, the camp director shares thoughts about Mattie's message of hope and peace, and his love for life and laughter and "playing after the storm." The campers then take turns affixing the "Sacred Monkey" to their wheelchairs, and taking pride in their opportunity to seek homage for this camp icon.

"HOW THE STARS CAME TO BE
AT CAMP MARIA"
BY MATTIE J.T. STEPANEK, JUNE 17, 2000

Once upon a time there was a group of very special children. They laughed and cried and played and slept like other children. And yet this group of children was special in a unique way.

For one thing, this group of children knew all about some words that other children never even heard of. Words like Duchenne, Becker, spinal muscular atrophy, Friedreich's ataxia, Charcot-Marie-Tooth, limb-girdle, and mitochondrial myopathy. They also knew words like braces, wheelchairs, bipap machines, nebulizers, steroids, muscle cramps, and life expectancy.

Another thing that made this group of children very special was that they understood about feelings. They understood very intense feelings. Feelings like fear, sadness, frustration, anger, and loss. And feelings like hope, trust, optimism, and resiliency. What was really neat was that some of these children didn't even know what the words describing these feelings meant, but they understood what the feelings were like, because they lived with those feelings every year.

Well, one day, a long time ago, yet not so long ago at all, something very, very special happened for this group of very special children. Some very special grown-ups, who were something like magical angels on earth, got together and decided that unique children needed a unique place to get together. They needed to get together to get to know each other, and they needed to get to know about being independent, and they needed to get to know how much fun life can really be. The grown-ups decided that the children who knew the big words and understood the intense feelings would spend a week at Camp Maria, doing nothing but celebrating the gift of life.

When the children arrived at Camp Maria for the very first time, they didn't know quite what to expect. They were told that Camp Maria was all about "Friends Helping Friends." And across the week, they went swimming and boating, and they did arts and crafts and made little race cars, and they played wheelchair football and baseball. There was singing and dancing. There were campfires. There was karaoke. In fact, by the end of the week, these children who weren't quite sure what to expect looked back at their week at Camp Maria and already began to miss all the activities and people. They all understood what "Friends Helping Friends" really meant.

When it was almost time for these unique and special children to leave for home, the magical angels asked them each to say or write a wish onto a little piece of paper. They were told that the little pieces of paper would be put into a basket tied to balloons. The basket would then float up into the heavens, and even if the wishes didn't come true in the exact way they were wished for, the magic of wishing would bring hope to the children.

The grown-ups told the children that they would know that their wishes were bringing hope to them, and to the whole world, each time they looked up into the sky of a clear night. They told them that each wish became a special star that shined brightly in the sky, and in the hearts of all children and grown-ups who believe in hope. The children were very, very excited.

Some of the children wished for things like a new puppy, or Pokémon cards, or a really cool CD. Some of the children wished for things like a new wheelchair that had a motor, or a really long straw to make drinking easier, or a laptop computer. Some of the children wished for things like world peace, or to have their books of poetry published, or for a baby brother or sister. And even though they didn't write it down, all of the children wished in their hearts that one day, all children would still be special, but that no child would ever have to be special for knowing about big words like muscular dystrophy, or for understanding intense feelings like worrying about the future.

When all of the little pieces of paper were placed into the balloon basket, the children cheered and smiled as they watched their wishes slowly drift up into the heavens. And suddenly, something wonderful happened . . . all of these unique and special children could feel the hope of a thousand stars twinkling and shining all around them. They knew in their hearts that even though they would face many gray clouds in their lives, they would always remember to play after every storm.

This group of very unique and special children went home with a spirit that was even stronger than when they first came to Camp Maria. And every summer since then, more and more unique and special children, who know the big words and understand intense feelings, keep coming to Camp Maria to celebrate life. And all of the children who come to Camp Maria to celebrate the gift of life learn about "Friends Helping Friends." They learn about bringing out the best in themselves and in other people. They learn about how to feel the stars all around them that symbolize wishes and hopes. And most of all, they all understand that something good is happening to their spirits, and they live hopefully ever after. And that is the story of "How the Stars Came to Be at Camp Maria."

Mattie (third from left) surrounded by some of his "Martin Ladies" (members of the girls' Martin cabin) at Camp Maria, in Leonardtown, Maryland, June 2002.

When I was running for governor a number of years ago, my wife and I didn't have much money, so we traveled around the state and we estimated later that we shook hands personally with 600,000 people.

Later I ran for president, as some of you may remember, and campaigned in all fifty states. Subsequently, I traveled around the world. In fact, since I left the White House, my wife and I have been to more than 120 nations. And we have known kings and queens, and we've known presidents and prime ministers, but the most extraordinary person whom I have ever known in my life is Mattie Stepanek.

I didn't know Mattie until about three years ago when [Children's National Medical Center] sent me a letter and said there was a little boy who only had a few more days to live and his final request was to meet Jimmy Carter. I was surprised and honored and within a few days [I called him in the ICU. Several months later], as a matter of fact, the *Good Morning America* program arranged for Mattie to be interviewed and for me to come there as a surprise to meet with him. He later told his mother, Jeni, that when I walked in the room he thought it was a presidential impersonator. And later, when it proved to be me, he told Jeni, and Jeni told me, that that was the first time in his life, and maybe the only time, when Mattie was speechless. But we exchanged greetings and formed, I would say, an instantaneous bond of love.

The next morning back home, Mattie woke up and he told Jeni what a wonderful time he had had. He had been dreaming, but he was so proud that he had met Jimmy Carter. And Jeni, often teasing Mattie, said, "Mattie, you must have been dreaming. You haven't actually met Jimmy Carter," and Mattie burst into tears and Jeni very quickly reassured him that we had actually had a personal meeting.

That meeting and our subsequent relationship have literally changed my life for the better. Mattie said that day that I had been his hero for a long time and I was sure that he was just joking and he could tell on the ABC program that I didn't really quite believe him. And so to prove that, he sent me a video, a twenty-minute-long video that he had made when he was seven years old, explaining the life of Jimmy Carter. And for the different segments in the video, he dressed appropriately.

So, it started out I was a little farm boy and Mattie had on ragged clothes and he spoke with what Rosalynn and I thought was an atrocious Southern accent. And then later I was a naval officer and then later I came back to be a farmer and then ultimately was president, so he changed clothes every time. And then while I was president, he gave an appeal to human rights and peace and things of that kind and while the camera was on him, he realized later, his toes kept wiggling, he was barefoot, so for a long time he apologized to me that he should have done that segment over and at least put on shoes to be president.

He sent me another video, which I would like for all of you to try to see. It's a video of his competition as a black belt in martial arts for the ultimate prize in that intense and demanding sport. It was incredible to see the agility of that young boy and the strength in his body.

Mattie and I began to correspond. After his death, Jeni gave me the honor of letting me come and do this speech. I had my secretary get out our correspondence. It's [inches] thick, on every possible subject. He was always in some degree of anguish, and I think embarrassment, when his books on the New York Times list were always above mine. And he would sympathize with me and say, "Well, you know, maybe poetry just has less competition than what you are writing about." But he was very sensitive to my feelings.

We also were close enough for Mattie to share some of his problems with me in his private messages. He talked about when he and Jeni were not well off and some local churches, I'm sure not the one represented here this morning, would take up a food collection and send it to them. Mattie used to examine the labels on the food and quite often he said he would find that the date had expired and that people were giving poor people inferior food that they didn't want to use themselves. And Mattie said, "If my books make a lot of money, we're going to get food that's brand new and make sure that poor people get the best food, even if we have to eat the old, outdated food in our house." He was very proud of the fact that he and his mother could move into a place that had windows.

I've thought a lot about Mattie's religious faith. It's all-encompassing, to include all human beings who believe in peace and justice and humility and service and compassion and love. The exact characteristics of our Savior Jesus Christ. He was still a boy, although he had the mind and the consciousness and the awareness of global affairs of a mature, philosophical adult.

One of his prime goals in life was to see the movie *Return of the King* seven times and I hope he was able to accomplish his goal. I'm not quite sure. But that was the kind of thing that he had as his ambitions.

He was as proud as I was when I won the Nobel Peace Prize, which has already been mentioned. As soon as the ceremony was over at the hall in Oslo, I went by myself to the top of a little hill right behind the place and I found a rock and I inscribed on it and I sent it to Mattie, because I felt that he shared the honor that I had received.

The last few days, I have been rereading some of Mattie's statements that he wrote to me, I've reread the correspondence. One thing he said was, "I choose to live until death, not spend the time dying until death occurs."

Jeni told me about one occasion when Mattie was supposed to be a main part of the program which he helped prepare to raise funds for muscular dystrophy, but when the time approached he was in the intensive care unit. They announced at first that Mattie could not attend the event that meant so much to him, in which he had helped in its preparation. He insisted on coming. When he got there and began to say his lines, he announced, "I'm out of breath. I can't speak." Mattie loved to dress up and to wear fancy clothes and his favorite kind of fancy clothes, as some of you may surmise, was a tuxedo. So [MDA] arranged for him to put on a tuxedo and he said, "When I have a tuxedo on, I can [breathe better]." So he went back with his tuxedo.

Mattie said he wanted to be, as an ultimate goal in his life, an ambassador of humanity and a daddy. Mattie had already named his first seven children and had even given personal idiosyncrasies and characteristics to the first four. He wanted to leave a human legacy and family descendants, but Mattie's legacy, obviously, is much greater than that.

As has already been quoted, he said, "I want to be [remembered as] a poet, a peacemaker, and a philosopher who played." Mattie was deeply aware of international affairs and shared a lot of his thoughts with me. He was once again in the intensive care unit when the war in Iraq began and Mattie burst into uncontrollable sobs of grief and anger. Jeni said he had never cried nearly so much about his own health or his own problems.

He wrote me right after that and I will quote exactly what he said: "Dear Jimmy, I am hurting about the war and I cried last night when I saw the attack on Iraq. I am not trying to be disrespectful, but I feel like [the] decision [was made] long ago that [we were] going to have this war, and [people have] spent so much energy carving out the trench that would support [this] plan. Imagine if [they] had spent as much time and energy considering the possibility of peace as [they have] convincing others of the inevitability of war. We'd be at a different point in history today."

Mattie was obviously extremely idealistic, but not completely idealistic. He also wrote me in a different letter, "I know that I should be peaceful with everyone, but it's also not smart," he said, "to put yourself in a dangerous situation. Like even though I would want to talk to Osama bin Laden about peace in the future, I wouldn't want to be alone with him in his cave." In the same letter he asked me if I would join him not just in that meeting, but in writing a book that Mattie wanted to call, and had already named, "Just Peace."

In an incredible way for a child his age, he analyzed the semantics of the word "just." The title was "Just Peace" and he said "just" had so many connotations that he thought that was the best word to put before "peace." He said "just" could be a minimal expectation, just peace, nothing else. It could mean just peace and peace as a paramount commitment, above everything else. And it could mean a peace that was exemplified by justice.

I spent seven years earlier in my life writing a book of poems about which Mattie was graciously complimentary. Poetry seemed to flow out of Mattie, kind of like an automatic stream, directed by inspiration through

Mattie's hands for the enjoyment of hundreds of thousands, maybe millions of people. I want to read just a few of them with which many of you are familiar, because he combined humor with serious thoughts. All of them I would say are unique, surprising when you read them.

One of them is entitled "About Angels" and he honored me by letting me write the foreword to this book, called *Journey Through Heartsongs* [Hyperion/VSP, 2002].

About Angels
Do you know what angels wear?
They wear
Angel-halos and Angel-wings, and
Angel-dresses and Angel-shirts under them, and
Angel-underwear and Angel-shoes and Angel-socks, and
On their heads
They wear
Angel-hair—
Except if they don't have any hair.
Some children and grown-ups
Don't have any hair because they
Have to take medicine that makes it fall out.
And sometimes,
The medicine makes them all better.
And sometimes,
The medicine doesn't make them all better,
And they die.
And they don't have any Angel-hair.
So do you know what God does then?
He gives them an
Angel-wig.
And that's what Angels wear.

I like them all, but there's another I would like to read.

Heavenly Greeting
Dear God,
For a long time,
I have wondered about
How You will meet me
When I die and come to
Live with You in Heaven.
I know You reach out
Your hand to welcome
Your people into Your home,
But I never knew if You
Reached out Your right hand,
Or if You
Reached out Your left hand.
But now I don't have to
Wonder about that anymore.
I asked my mommy and
She told me that You
Reach out both of Your hands,
And welcome us with
A great big giant hug.
Wow!
I can't wait for my hug, God.
Thank You,
And Amen.

And another one that he wrote:

I Could . . . If They Would
If they would find a cure when I'm a kid . . .
I could ride a bike and sail on rollerblades, and

I could go on really long nature hikes.
If they would find a cure when I'm a teenager . . .
I could earn my license and drive a car, and
I could dance every dance at my senior prom.
If they would find a cure when I'm a young adult . . .
I could travel around the world and teach peace, and
I could marry and have children of my own.
If they would find a cure when I'm grown old . . .
I could visit exotic places and appreciate culture, and
I could proudly share pictures of my grandchildren.
If they would find a cure when I'm alive . . .
I could live each day without pain and machines, and
I could celebrate the biggest thank you of life ever.
If they would find a cure when I'm buried into Heaven . . .
I could still celebrate with my brothers and sister there, and
I could still be happy knowing that I was part of the effort.

And the last poem I will read is entitled "When I Die (Part II)."

When I Die (Part II)

When I die, I want to be
A child in Heaven.
I want to be
A ten-year-old cherub.
I want to be
A hero in Heaven,
And a peacemaker,
Just like my goal on earth.
I will ask God if I can
Help the people in purgatory.
I will help them think,
About their life,
About their spirits,

About their future.
I will help them
Hear their own Heartsongs again,
So they can finally
See the face of God,
So soon.
When I die,
I want to be,
Just like I want to be
Here on earth.

Well, it's hard to know anyone who has suffered more than Mattie. Sandy [Newcomb, a dear family friend,] sent us almost daily reports about his bleeding, internally and from his fingers. I doubt that anyone in this great auditorium has ever suffered so much except his mother, Jeni, and our Savior Jesus Christ, who is also here with us today. I always saw the dichotomy between Mattie as a child and with the characteristics and intelligence and awareness of an adult. Just as we see the dichotomy of Jesus Christ who was fully a human being at the same time as truly God.

I would say that my final assessment is that Mattie was an angel. Someone said that to him once and he said, "No, no." He was very modest. But really in the New Testament language, angel and messenger are the same and there's no doubt that Mattie was an angel of God, a messenger of God.

He was concerned about his legacy, wanting to have seven children and talking about his grandchildren, but Mattie's legacy is forever because his Heartsongs will resonate in the hearts of people forever. I thank God that he is no longer suffering and that he's with the Prince of Peace, getting big hugs in Heaven, and maybe wearing a tuxedo.

Former President Jimmy Carter delivering the eulogy at Mattie's funeral Mass in Wheaton, Maryland, June 28, 2004. Behind him are Fr. Dominick Eshikena, Monsignor John Enzler, and Fr. Robert Mordino.

Mattie's casket is carried out of the church following his funeral Mass by his "kin"—Heather Dobbins (front L), Chris Dobbins (front R), Cynthia Dobbins (middle L), and Jamie Dobbins (middle R).

Mattie's fire fighter buddies "JJ" Jackson of Mississauga, Canada, and Bert "Bubba" Mentrassi of Greenburgh, New York, talk to Mattie during his "last ride." Mattie's casket was draped with a blue United Nations flag that had been flown during a peacekeeping mission in Kosovo.

Mattie's mom, Jeni, and his service dog, Micah, visiting the Gate of Heaven Cemetery in Silver Spring, Maryland, where Mattie is buried with his siblings, Katie, Stevie, and Jamie.

MATTIE'S LEGACY OF HOPE AND PEACE
BY JENI STEPANEK

Since Mattie's death, there have been many individuals and organizations endeavoring to commemorate Mattie's legacy of hope and peace in meaningful and lasting ways. The Muscular Dystrophy Association is committed to continuing Mattie's efforts to raise funds for MDA clinics and summer camp programs with his ongoing annual Heartsongs Gala, held every February in Washington, D.C. MDA has also created the MDA Mattie Fund to direct research dollars toward the neuromuscular diseases that take the lives of children, including mitochondrial myopathies like the one that led to the death of Mattie and his three siblings.

Scholarships and awards have been established in Mattie's honor, such as the Intergenerational Caregiving Scholarship, sponsored by the Rosalynn Carter Institute with the support of Johnson & Johnson, and the Mattie J.T. Stepanek Peacemaker Award, given annually by the We Are Family Foundation during its spring gala. The We Are Family Foundation, together with the Lollipop Theater Network, has also instituted "Mattie's Movie and Poetry Day" at numerous children's hospitals in the country.

The Children's Peace Pavilion in Independence, Missouri, is updating and expanding its entrance attraction, the Mattie J.T. Stepanek "Peace Is Possible" exhibit, which first opened in April 2004. CPP is also incorporating Mattie's message of hope from "Just Peace" in its curriculum and program development. Children's National Medical Center in Washington, D.C., Mattie's "home away from home" for many years, is continuing its efforts to secure funds and build a new state-of-the-science and state-of-the-art pediatric intensive care unit to be named in Mattie's honor, and Holy Rosary Catholic Church in Upper Marlboro, Maryland, the church Mattie attended during much of his life, has opened the Mattie J.T. Stepanek Memorial Library. A committee of children and adults has also formed to gather and present information to the Catholic Church for the cause of having Mattie formally recognized as a saint—"St. Mattie of Hope and Peace."

Perhaps one of the most visible and accessible efforts under way to commemorate Mattie's life as peacemaker is the development of a twenty-six-acre park, currently under construction in the Rockville, Maryland, neighborhood where Mattie lived. On June 18, 2005, more than 300 people gathered to celebrate the groundbreaking ceremony for the "Mattie J.T. Stepanek Park at King Farm." When completed, this fully accessible park and playground will include ball courts and fields, paths and meditation areas, and benches with inspirational quotes from Mattie's poetry. A central highlight of the park will be a life-size statue of Mattie in his wheelchair with his service dog, Micah, beside him, both of them sitting at a chess table with an empty bench on the opposite side. Nearby, a plaque inviting visitors to sit contemplatively for a moment will bear a quote from this book: "Peace is possible. It can begin simply, over a game of chess and a cup of tea."

Chris Cuomo delivers the keynote speech during the Third Annual Heartsongs Luncheon to benefit the new Pediatric Intensive Care Unit at Children's National Medical Center in Washington, D.C. The new unit, currently under funding and construction efforts, is being named in honor of Mattie, who spent many months at a time living in the older PICU at CNMC. Mattie helped the hospital staff in many fund-raising appeals seeking much-needed resources for this new state-of-the-science and state-of-the-art facility.

Mayor Larry Giamo describes Mattie as a "strong and inspirational spirit, who was a great citizen of Rockville, and a great citizen of the world" during the June 2005 ground-breaking ceremony for the twenty-six-acre "Mattie J.T. Stepanek Park at King Farm," Rockville, Maryland.

Kaylee Dobbins kisses a picture of her "Uncle Mattie" while Lt. Governor Michael S. Steele (R-MD) and Mattie's mom and service dog listen to the speeches by other politicians and dignitaries.

Mattie's mom, Jeni, and Mattie's "neighbor niece," Kaylee, break ground for the new "Mattie Park" along with Lt. Governor Michael S. Steele (R-MD), Congressman Chris Van Hollen (D-MD), and members of the Rockville City Council and the King Farm Citizens Association June 18, 2005.

Jeni, Kaylee Dobbins, and local and state representatives celebrate as the sign for "Mattie's Park" is unveiled.

Jeni and Micah admire the new sign announcing the naming of the "Mattie Park" with Andy Gordon, president of the King Farm Citizens Association, and Bert Hall, director of Parks and Recreation in Rockville, Maryland, and neighbor Bob Balkam, a strong advocate in designating the park as a commemoration of Mattie's life and legacy.

A bust of Mattie being created by sculptor Jimilu Mason © 2005. Jimilu is one of several artists who have submitted samples of their work for consideration as the statue of Mattie for the new park is being planned.

Bob and Margaret Beaver, Clifton Oden, and Alvin Turner (L to R) join Mattie's mom, Jeni, and Mattie's service dog, Micah, during the dedication of the new Mattie J.T. Stepanek Memorial Library at Holy Rosary Parish in Upper Marlboro, Maryland, June 2005. Mattie attended Holy Rosary most of his life and served as a Minister of the Word for the parish and a Sunday School teacher for second and sixth graders there. The committee gathering information for the cause of Mattie being formally recognized as "St. Mattie of Hope and Peace" by the Catholic Church was first formed at Holy Rosary by Mattie's peers, and has been joined by many other people across other parishes and faiths.

(L to R) Altar server Patrick O'Malley, Nathan Clavelli (Cub Scout Troop 1770), Timothy Clavelli (Boy Scout Troop 1575), Rosella Harris (Girl Scout Troop 0653), members of the Knights of Columbus Fourth Degree Ceremonial Team (Archdiocese of Washington, D.C.), and altar servers William Marshall and John Ferguson surround Fr. Isidore Dixon during the blessing and dedication of the magnolia tree planted at Holy Rosary Parish in Upper Marlboro, Maryland.

The magnolia tree and hand-carved sign at Holy Rosary that were dedicated in memory and honor of the first anniversary of Mattie's death, June 2005.

MDA National Spokesperson Jerry Lewis was very emotional when receiving his copy of *Reflections of a Peacemaker: A Portrait Through Heartsongs* from Mattie's mom, Jeni, with a special bookplate in the front, signed by Mattie for his good friend and "advocate hero." Mattie signed the bookplates before he died, knowing that he would probably not be here when his final collection of poetry was released. Mattie also created a special stamp with his signature and a message from him, to be used during book signings for his last two manuscripts after his death.

Mattie's friend Sean Astin (aka the hobbit Samwise from *The Lord of the Rings* movies), putting Mattie's special stamp into copies of *Reflections of a Peacemaker* during a Los Angeles book signing just after the release of Mattie's final new book of poetry, August 2005. Sean promised Mattie that he would spread his message of hope and peace in honor of him, and has remained active in carrying on with Mattie's mission of humanitarian and peacemaking efforts.

Mattie's mom, Jeni, and Mattie's service dog, Micah, get ready for their first hometown book signing of Mattie's new poetry book in Rockville, Maryland, in September 2005. *Reflections of a Peacemaker* became a *New York Times* best-seller when it was released a year after Mattie's death. A portion of the proceeds from the book go to the MDA Mattie Fund.

Madison Cross during her debut concert performance of the single "He Was Just Like Me,"
a song written by her father, Grammy- and
Oscar Award–winning artist Christopher Cross,
as a tribute to Mattie. Mattie became close
friends with Madison and her family, and they
traveled frequently from L.A. to spend time with
Mattie, visiting him in the hospital, attending
his MDA Heartsongs Gala, and celebrating
birthdays. One hundred percent of the proceeds of the single and iTunes download of this
song, which has been featured on Radio
Disney, goes to support the MDA Mattie Fund.

IAFF General President Harold
Schaitberger and Lynnco Custom
Cycles President Lynn Jones
meet with Mattie's mom, Jeni, at
the IAFF headquarters in
Washington, D.C., in October
2005 to discuss plans for "The
Peacemaker Bike" that will honor
Mattie's legacy of hope and
peace. Lynnco is designing a bike with a Harley-Davidson engine that
will be donated to the IAFF to raise funds for the MDA Mattie Fund.
The motorcycle will feature icons related to Mattie's message and a
silhouette of Mattie's face, and it will integrate his love for fire fighters
and bikers and life.

One of artist Cyril Huze's many sketches
for possible designs that will become
"The Peacemaker Bike" honoring
Mattie's life and supporting the MDA
Mattie Fund, which was created on June
22, 2004, and raised $1.5 million in the
year and a half after Mattie's death.
Lynnco and IAFF hope that this bike will
raise another $2 million for the fund,
which supports research in childhood
neuromuscular diseases like the one
that affected Mattie.

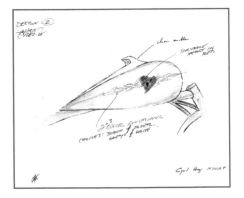

Eternal Echoes

Our life is an echo
Of our spirit today,
Of our essence
As it is,
Caught between
Our yesterday
And our tomorrow.
It is the resounding
Reality of who we are,
As a result of
Where we have been,
And where we will be
For eternity.

By Mattie J.T. Stepanek, May 14, 2000,
in *Journey Through Heartsongs*
(Hyperion/VSP, 2002)